Faith.

From the Journal of Umm Zakiyyah

Faith. From the Journal of Umm Zakiyyah
By Umm Zakiyyah

Copyright © 2016 by Al-Walaa Publications.
All Rights Reserved.

ISBN: 978-1-942985-10-5
Library of Congress Control Number: 2016963513

Order information at ummzakiyyah.com/store

Verses from Qur'an adapted from Saheeh International, Darussalam, and Yusuf Ali translations.

Published by Al-Walaa Publications
Camp Springs, Maryland USA

Cover photo credit: Shutterstock © by Laboo Studio

Contents.

Preface

Author's Note.	4
Dedication.	5
Qur'an.	6
Du'aa.	7
Hearts.	8
Paths.	32
Fear.	59
Prayer.	72
Patience.	84
Religion.	100
Ihsaan.	121
Also by Umm Zakiyyah	143
Glossary of Arabic Terms	144
About the Author	146

Author's Note.

Ahlul-Qiblah.
"It is they for whom the flag of Paradise was raised and they raced to earn it, and the Straight Path was laid for them and they took it firmly. They believed that it was great error to sell what no eye has seen, no ear has heard and no heart has imagined of delight in the eternal dwelling, in return for a perishable life that passes as fast as a dream and is full of grief and depression. If this life makes one laugh a little, it also brings one many instances of crying, and if it delighted for a day, it would cause grief for months... this life goes on with various fears and ends in certain demise."
—from **Establish the Prayers and the Prize is Paradise by Abdul-Malik Al-Qasim**

I've written so much in my journal about faith that I wouldn't know where to begin explaining the inspiration behind this work. So I pray in its words is an explanation all its own.

But suffice it to say, when it comes to faith, I'm still learning. So I claim no authority except that I hope to die with more than a grain of it in my heart.

This collection is just a glimpse into my world of hope and confusion as I strive upon that path.

*For the spiritual prisoners in this world.
May Paradise be your release.*

Dedication.

Qur'an.

"Then do you remember Me, I will remember you. Be grateful to Me. And do not disbelieve."
—*Al-Baqarah,* **2:152**

~

"And let not their speech grieve you. Indeed, honor belongs to Allah entirely. He is the Hearing, All-Knowing."
—*Yunus,* **10:65**

O Allah, Al-Wadood, Ar-Rahmaan! Remember me when I forget You. Have mercy on me when I don't have mercy on myself. And O Allah, Al-Haadiy, Ar-Rasheed! Pull me back to right guidance even when I seek misguidance. And remind me that I am Your servant when I forget myself. And O Allah, Al-Wahhaab, Ar-Razzaaq! Remove the dunya from my heart, and place it in my hand.

Du'aa.

Hearts.

From the Journal of Umm Zakiyyah

Courage.

Courage is the willingness to make mistakes and self-correct, and to do it continuously.
Faith is trusting that your Lord will forgive you each time you fall, so long as you keep getting up and trying again.
The person who is unwilling to take any risk has neither courage nor faith.

~

Pride destroys courage and makes for toxic relationships—with the self and others. Surround yourself with those courageous enough to see their pain and to seek help in working through it.

~

Beware of controlled humility and detached accountability. Controlled humility is when you are able to admit your faults only when you see them first, but not when someone brings them to your attention. Detached accountability is when you accept that a negative observation of you is correct, but only in past tense.
Thus, you are consistently able to reflect on times past and say, "Looking back, I can see I was wrong." But you are utterly incapable of saying with any honesty or sincerity, "I am wrong now."
In other words, you see your wrongs only when there's absolutely nothing to do about them right now.
Both controlled humility and detached accountability are symptoms of a heart reeking of destructive pride and self-deception.

Words.

Even when your heart feels dead, keep your tongue alive with *dhikr*. It may become the resuscitation of your heart.

~

If you want your Lord to speak good words about you above the heavens, then speak good words about His believers on earth. If you want your Lord to have mercy on you, then have mercy on His servants in this world. If you want His angels to speak your name in their prayers, then speak the names of fellow Muslims in yours. If you want
Al-Wadood, The Loving, to cover your faults, pardon your errors, and forgive your sins, then rush to cover, pardon, and forgive your brothers and sisters in this world.

~

If someone wants to think good of you, they will. It really is that simple, *bi'idhnillaah*. It's not upon you to explain yourself to their satisfaction. It's upon them to make excuses for you to Allah's satisfaction.

Beauty.

I love beautiful people. I don't mean the ones with perfect physiques and a thousand poses "on fleek." I mean the ones who make you smile so wide that tears fill your eyes just from the joy your soul feels at being in their presence. They remind you of Allah and the Hereafter; they remind you of your imminent death and accountability for your deeds. Yet still, they find a way to make you laugh from that deep place inside, and you find yourself constantly looking forward to when you'll see them again.

O Allah, place us in righteous company,
and make us righteous company!
And take our souls in a state most pleasing to You!

Anxiety.

If something is troubling you to the point of anxiety and frustration because you have no idea how things will end up, then look to three things: your heart, your tongue, and your hands.

If your heart is repentant and patient, if your tongue is uttering prayers of forgiveness and God's praise, and if your hands are busy with good, then receive glad tidings, *bi'idhnillah*. For your Lord says, "Is there any reward for good except good?"

But if your heart is restless and impatient, if your tongue is uttering angry outbursts and complaints, and if your hands are busy with sin, then woe to you. You should stop and repent—and still receive glad tidings, for your Lord says, "I am All-Forgiving, Most Merciful."

Reminders.

When we are doing wrong, Allah afflicts us with guilt, thereby calling us back to Him. Yet some of us fight this internal reminder by using our tongues to defend our wrong, hoping to quiet the guilt and convince ourselves that we are right.

Then Allah uses the tongues of others, thereby calling us back to Him. Yet some of us fight this external reminder by using the same arguments we used to quiet our guilt—or by pointing out the faults of the one who is speaking. "They're being judgmental!" we say. "They have no wisdom or compassion!" We then arrogantly return to wrong, justifying our sin because of the faults we see in those who heeded the advice of their Lord, "And remind, for verily the reminder benefits the believers" (51:55).

Yet Allah continues to call us back to Him, as our hearts are continuously afflicted with guilt, and the tongues of others continuously remind us of our wrongs. Yet so many of us relentlessly fight the internal and external reminders...until our hearts become deaf to both.

Then Allah afflicts us with the harshest lesson—that of life itself—sending into our lives the storms of suffering in response to our sins. And only then, for so many of us, do our hearts hear for the first time Allah's call. But even in this, there is mercy.

For surely, those who ignore the mercy of Allah—manifested in the internal and external reminders of guilt, others' words, and the storms of life—have only Allah Himself as their teacher, when He calls them back to Him one final time.

Drowning.

Heart Break.

"And like the water that breaks the boat, when the dunya enters, it shatters our heart."—Yasmin Mogahed

Self-deception is one of the fastest ways to break your own boat—and drown yourself and those who trusted you to guide them to the shore.
What is self-deception? It is "the good cause."
It is busying yourself with charity and community work but being too busy to *every day* read and reflect on Qur'an, or to pray on time and with concentration.
It is becoming so consumed with "necessary" projects and activism that you begin to understand your obligation to Allah only through their lens, instead of understanding them only through the lens of your obligation to Allah.
It is convincing yourself that Islam needs you instead of the other way around. So in the name of *da'wah* or "normalizing Islam," you'll do whatever *feels right* to you, even if it is sinful or harmful to your soul or the souls of others.
It is telling yourself that you only wish to spread good on earth, while you are in fact spreading corruption. And it is thinking you are earning good deeds while you are really on a path to Hellfire…
All because you never fortified your spiritual "boat" in the first place—through connecting daily to Allah through Qur'an, *Salaah*, and *du'aa*…and sincerely seeking the advice of—or humbly listening to—the believers whom Allah sent to save you from drowning.

"And when it is said to them, 'Make not mischief on the earth,' they say, 'We are only peacemakers.' Verily, they are the ones who make mischief but they perceive not" (*Al-Baqarah*, 2:11-12).

"Say, 'Shall We tell you the greatest losers with respect to [their] deeds? Those whose efforts have been wasted in this life while they thought they were acquiring good by their work…" (*Al-Kahf*, 18:103-104).

May Allah protect us from being amongst them!

One Body.

The ummah is one body. If one part of it hurts, the rest hurts. We often think this concerns only the harm that others inflict on us. But it also concerns the harm we inflict on ourselves—intentionally or unintentionally.

Just as with your physical body, you cannot wound one part of it and imagine that the other parts have no "right" to feel hurt.

Pain isn't a choice. It's a natural response to being hurt. And when we are hurt, we have not only the right, but the obligation to seek healing.

Our *emaan* is like the nerves in the human body.

The stronger and healthier they are, the more we feel when something is wrong. The weaker and less functional they are, the less we feel when something is wrong.

Continuous sin and wrongdoing—and our collective approval of it, whether in the name of progress, political gain, or individual choice—causes long term "nerve damage."

That's why so many of us don't *feel* anymore. And we can actually spend more time arguing about whether or not these feelings should exist than finding ways to seek healing.

A heart that blames others is a heart that has not learned of itself.

~

Entitlement and empathy are mutually exclusive. Our hearts can house only one at a time.

~

Any of us can speak in a soft voice, but that doesn't mean we have soft hearts—or tongues.

Empathy.

Self-Deception.

You can only lie to yourself but for so long, before your heart cries out and demands to bear witness.

~

Sometimes the "crabs in the bucket" are in your own mind—preventing you from the greatness that God has in store for you.

~

When your heart loathes something, the mere mention of it evokes the worst possible image, then your mind defines it as such. Thus, even in the face of obvious good or in a wholly unrelated context, your internal loathing moves you to mention the potential (or present) deplorable "nature" of that thing.

This is why so many people speak ill of Islam in contexts praising the achievements of individual Muslims, and this is why so many Muslims speak ill of divorce and plural marriage in contexts mentioning the necessity and good of their personal practice.

We cannot sit still upon hearing the good of these mercies from Allah, because our ailing hearts do not allow us to. Yet ironically, like the Islamophobe who cannot be quiet about the "crimes" of professed Muslims, we truly imagine that our consistent verbal negativity on these subjects is rooted in wanting to fight corruption and wrongdoing on earth.

Polygyny.

Why do we always apologize or offer disclaimers whenever we speak positively about polygyny, saying quickly, "But it's not for everyone." Do we apologize and offer disclaimers when we speak positively about monogamy, saying hurriedly, "But it's not for everyone."

Yet both are equally true. So why the double standard? I think marriage itself is self-evident in the fact that no one's individual choice is for everyone. So why state the obvious? As I say often, "Usually, when we state the obvious, it's for a reason other than the obvious."

Is it that you believe Allah's religion needs your apology and disclaimers? If so, remember, Allah's religion doesn't even need *you*.

So be careful how you speak about the gift of Islam your Lord has given you. Like life itself, this gift can be taken from you at any moment. Don't play with it.

So dear soul, watch yourself—and limit your apologies and disclaimers to when you're speaking about *your own* faults and shamefulness.

Islam has neither.

Frustration.

If you find yourself angry or frustrated with God, then there is a deep spiritual sickness in your heart that has led you to believe that God is your servant instead of the other way around.

God is not our personal bank teller or wish granter.

Yes, we call on Him and He responds to our prayers. But prayers are not demands. They are sincere, humble requests beseeching The Most Generous, the One who showers blessings upon us while we've done nothing to deserve them. Thus, to become angry or frustrated when we don't get what we want isn't too different from a child having a tantrum when his or her parents don't bestow every coveted prize or toy. Dear soul, you need to take an honest look at what you understand your purpose of life to be, then feel anger and frustration—and happiness—to the extent that you fulfill that.

Ignorance.

There is a level of ignorance that could never be addressed with words.
This is the type of ignorance born of either a heart that is spiritually sick, or a life lacking significant experience.
So I'm beginning to understand more and more the wisdom of the Qur'anic instruction to say only, "Peace" to the ignorant, and keep it moving.

~

A glaring sign of religious ignorance under the guise of knowledge is teaching believers to view spirituality through the lens of their relationship with certain people instead of their relationship with Allah. Righteous scholars simply do not do this, because Islam does not do this. And righteous scholars teach Islam.

~

How we've reached a level of ignorance and misguidance that we now claim certain people are infallible is beyond me.
This was never claimed of even the most honorable of the Prophet's Companions. What on earth possesses us to think it can be claimed of *anyone* from amongst us?
No matter how "honorable" we imagine them to be.

The Battlefield.

Do not enter marriage like one enters a battlefield, equipped with all the necessary weapons to win a war against an adversary whom you are convinced is wishing you harm. Marriage isn't where you "fight" for your rights. It's where you lay down all the weapons, shields, and pretenses you needed out in the world so that you can now allow your *libaas* to cover and shield you—like the Prophet (peace be upon him) begged of Khadijah (may Allah be pleased with her) when he was deeply shaken after receiving revelation for the first time. "Cover me, cover me," he begged. And she covered him.

So if you walk into the fortress of your home and feel the need to cover and shield yourself—after receiving the terrifying revelation that this life is full of trials and confusion—then something is very, very wrong.

A battle should never be plotted and waged within the protective walls of a fortress—unless an enemy has crossed the threshold.

So if you are preparing for battle each time your cross the threshold of your home, find out where the enemy is and how he got inside. And whether you find that he is *Shaytaan* or the one within yourself, use all the weapons you thought you needed to battle your loved one, and fight and expel this enemy instead.

~

Angry with someone and want to teach them a lesson they'll never forget? Before you rush to fill your Book of Deeds with vengeful words and deeds, consider carefully whether you're putting yourself on a battlefield opposite your Creator.

In a Qudsi hadith, Prophet Muhammad (peace be upon him) said that Allah has said, "Whoever shows enmity to someone devoted to Me, I shall be at war with him..." (Bukhari).

And given that someone's sincere devotion to Allah is largely a matter of the unseen, I think it's safest to devote your own self to Allah. And trust that He's fully capable of teaching His servants important lessons without your help.

True Love.

"If you truly cared, you would've never left!" or "A good friend will always be there, no matter what," we say.
But is it true?
These claims might make us feel self-righteous when loved ones walk away, but in truth, they're self-serving and dishonest.
It's possible that the person left simply because they prioritized their physical, emotional, and spiritual health over our company—no matter how much they loved and cared for us.

We hear a lot about toxic relationships and the importance of letting go, but it's rare that we turn that logic around and take an honest look at ourselves: Yes, it's possible that *you* are toxic to someone you love.

So if they truly care, they'll never leave?
No, this couldn't be further from the truth.
Rather, if they truly care—for their soul—they'll do all they can to protect it, even if it means walking away from someone they love and care for more than life itself.

~

A heart full of resentment is a heart incapable of love.

~

Waste not your time chasing a heart that is enclosed in a body other than your own.

Divine Love.

Love what Allah loves and strive upon the path to Paradise. This is how you gain His love. Never imagine that you understand the path to Allah's pleasure better than He does.

~

Some Muslims say we shouldn't strive for Paradise, we should strive for Allah's love. But is it even possible to seek one without the other?
We cannot strive for Paradise except that we live according to what Allah loves. And we cannot live according to what Allah loves without striving upon the path to Paradise.
And no, you cannot have a heart full of love for Allah unless you have a heart full of love for what He loves. And Allah loves the *Siraatul-Mustaqeem*, the path to Paradise. So strive upon it, dear believer. It is how you gain Allah's love.

~

Trivializing the importance of Paradise as a motivator in doing good deeds for the sake of Allah is treading dangerously close to trivializing the importance of Allah's Words themselves.
For it is Allah who promised believers Paradise in the Qur'an as encouragement for their striving on earth. For a human to then come after Him and say this motivation is misguided is a form of misguidance itself. Striving for Paradise and sincerely seeking the Pleasure and Love of Allah are not mutually exclusive. They are one and the same.
In Islam, a good deed is not a good deed unless it is done purely for the sake of Allah—and this includes doing good deeds in hope of entering Paradise.

Showing Off.

Every good deed announced publicly isn't "showing off." Actions are by intention, and some Muslims intend to speak regularly about their praying, fasting, and charity so that these good deeds are revived as normal amongst Muslims today.

And there are *many* who benefit from these reminders. Allah Himself speaks highly of charity given openly and secretly (13:22). So who are we to declare the ill intentions behind a believer's good deed, just because they spoke of it openly?

This declaration is in itself evil.

Not only are we speaking on behalf of Allah, declaring what is in the hearts of His believing servants, but we are also potentially slandering a servant of Allah for something that may earn them Paradise!

How do we know that Allah didn't accept their good deed announced publicly, while He rejected ours done under the veil of secrecy?

And even if our quietly-kept good deeds are accepted, by wronging a fellow believer, we could be cancelling even these as we seek to stop believers from speaking about theirs.

In the eyes of those who seek fault, no good you do is sincere, and any bad you do reflects who you "really" are.

~

Hypocrite or sincere repentant?
What you say about someone's positive changes after living a sinful life says more about your heart than theirs.

~

Think good of Allah, and He will become for you what you think He is. Expect good from Allah, and He will grant for you what you expect from Him. Then think good of yourself, expecting only the best for your life and soul.
How could you not—if you truly think and expect good of your Lord, who you trusted will grant it to you?

Sin.

Sins are subtle yet visceral assaults upon the soul.

~

Beware, though we all sin and are in need of Allah's mercy, sin should not be taken lightly. Sin is destructive to your life and soul, and it is destructive to your character and sanity. Sin without repentance is like terminal illness without treatment. In the early stages, the disease of sin (like the disease of the body) is barely detectable. But as it progresses, it obstructs the very life veins of spiritual life.

By Allah, a person cannot indulge in open, unrepentant sin except that he or she falls seriously ill, spiritually and mentally. And every part of the body bears testimony to the ailing of the spirit. The tongue becomes diseased and speaks lies as truth. The eyes become blurred and see darkness as light. The hands reach frantically for that which would wreak only more havoc to the spirit—and the limbs fall in submission. The mind caves in illness, convinced that evil is good. And the heart becomes hardened and rusted, until it cries out in conviction to its life of sin, "Ah! You are my Lord, and I am your servant!"

~

Some people do not want the good. They want what they want. And fulfilling their desires is the beginning and end of life for them. But they call it "following your heart."

If you remove the humility, you remove the beauty—and the benefit.

~

"How can sin draw you closer to Allah?" During my studies, an Islamic teacher asked us this question. We had just learned that *emaan* increases with obedience to Allah and decreases with disobedience, so we found the question confusing. Then she explained that a person may sin, but their subsequent regret and repentance thereafter can draw them so close to Allah that their *emaan* actually becomes stronger than before committing the sin.
This lesson stayed with me.
Today I see an even deeper lesson.
In my experience, many Muslims who are committing no obvious sin but are actively learning about Islam or teaching it, tend to be the *least* receptive to reminders about their souls and exhortations to fear Allah—particularly when the reminders come from someone they deem as "ignorant" or "sinful."
They often speak about Allah as if He and they are One. Thus, any disagreement with something they say or anyone offering a different perspective, is viewed as opposing Allah Himself—even when the other person's view is backed by Qur'an and Sunnah evidences. It often doesn't even *occur* to them to think, "What does Allah want me to learn from this person?"
It's quite terrifying to witness.
But many who are involved in obvious sin but are actively praying to Allah and feeling ashamed of their faults, tend to be very receptive to reminders about their souls and exhortations to fear Allah. The humility they display at the mere mention of Allah is quite humbling.
And it reminds me of the question my teacher asked.
How can sin draw you closer to Allah?
And the answer I have today is this: It can keep you ever aware that you are in desperate need of Allah's mercy and forgiveness, while viewing yourself as a "practicing Muslim" or a "teacher of Islam" can make you imagine you need to help *others* draw closer to Allah.

We'll never learn to truly love for the sake of Allah until we make a daily commitment to purify our hearts from the diseases of pride and *hasad*—destructive envy. If you imagine that one or both do not affect you, then you are likely suffering from these diseases the most. No heart is guaranteed protection from any spiritual ailment, no matter how righteous or "pure." For the purest hearts are pure precisely because they remain aware of the ever-present possibility of corruption, as no pure heart would ever confidently declare that it is pure.

~

Spiritual diseases, like physical diseases, in the earliest stages manifest in the subtlest, most undetectable ways. Yet it is a rather obvious symptom of spiritual corruption to imagine that only others suffer from the diseases of destructive pride and envy in their lives.

~

"I don't understand envy and jealousy," my friend said. Her words scared me because *hasad* and other diseases of the heart are most harmful when we think we're *not* experiencing them. Like Satan himself, *hasad* isn't a clear voice saying, "I'm evil and would love for you to destroy yourself and those around you. Do you accept my invitation to Hellfire?" Instead, these spiritual diseases manifest themselves as the most rational thinking and behavior while we're convinced we're right.

~

The heart tarnished with the deepest envy is blind to its own rust. So it sees its dislike for someone only through the lens of what that person has said or done, but almost never through the lens of its own sight-altering spiritual disease, *hasad*.

Compromise.

We like to refer to the prophetic example in times like this, especially when advocating for compromises in our faith under the guise of "compassion and tolerance." But let's not forget, our prophet of mercy was slandered, boycotted, fought, and called horrible names too, even as he did everything possible to show compassion and tolerance as he spoke the truth.

But it wasn't his compassion and tolerance that they had a problem with. It was his truth. God's truth.

During his era, the disbelievers would've been more than happy for him to leave off compassion and tolerance, if it meant giving up Islam and following their belief systems. After all, they certainly left off compassion and tolerance when dealing with *him*.

So no, it never was about compassion and tolerance. It was about playing politics and word games to make good appear evil, and truth appear false.

Nothing has changed.

They didn't want his compassion and tolerance—and they don't want ours. They want our hearts and souls. (And sadly, some of us are giving it to them.)

Yes, we will continue to show compassion and tolerance. Because it is what God instructs of us.

And it's the right thing to do.

But at a certain point, you're going to have to accept that it really doesn't matter whether or not others are pleased with you. Let it suffice that your Lord is pleased with you.

So leave them to their name-calling, slandering, and political word games. It's all they have. This is their Paradise, after all. Yours is in the Hereafter—if you want it.

Don't sacrifice it for the fleeting comfort and disingenuous acceptance they offer to you on earth.

So many people reject God and religion, allegedly because of all the harm done in its name. They wish to root out the cause of evil on earth, they say.

So I imagine it's only a matter of time—given all their advances in human intelligence—before they discover the true cause of the evil they see: the human being and its diseased heart.

I wonder how it will look when they try to root these out too, when their delusion leads them to reject another inalterable truth: their association with the species of humans on earth.

~

The refusal (or fear) to face oneself is at the root of much destructive pride and vicious scapegoating. These people are so terrified of the ugly truth of themselves that the only way they can cope is by convincing themselves that others are far beneath them, and that others are to blame for their own suffering and the suffering in the world.

All humans struggle with battling the self, but those who refuse to face themselves imagine that even the internal enemy (and thus the internal battle) is someone else's doing. Thus, when they suffer spiritual crisis, as many people do, they have no tools to self-correct because they imagine themselves to be victims within their own heart and soul. Thus, they often proclaim that God and religion—or Islam itself—is the culprit, so they abandon authentic spirituality in favor of a belief system that codifies the destructive pride and vicious scapegoating they've used all along to run from the truth of themselves. Only now, they view even the Creator as beneath them, and they blame Him and His religion for their own suffering and the suffering in the world.

Traps and Discord

We often caution each other to avoid discord, lest we fall victim to the traps of *Shaytaan*. But we must remember that, at times, *Shaytaan* is behind much of what we call love and harmony.

In today's world, it's become quite commonplace to support wrongdoing in the name of kindness, patience, and tolerance. But, as believers, our ultimate goal is not to avoid discord and hurting people's feelings.

It's to avoid discord with Allah and hurting our souls.

~

What could be more tragic than building our own prison then each day sharpening the weapon we'll use against ourselves? By Allah, this is what we're doing when we silence in even our closest circles any voice of dissent, criticism, or admonition lest it hurt our pride or threaten the comfortable existence we've built for ourselves.

We as parents, spouses, and religious leaders build these self-imposed prisons every day, then call it "disrespect" should any loved one whom we deem beneath us seek to remove the self-destructive weapon from our hands.

Paths.

From the Journal of Umm Zakiyyah

Time.

To value time is to value your soul.

~

In the end, your failures and successes in life—and ultimately in the Hereafter—boil down to one simple matter: how you spend your time.

~

Life is but a series of breaths, each one counting down to the very last.

~

I've learned that a "good heart" is one that always makes time for Allah, and learns to say no to people.
Being "busy" isn't a bad thing—if you're busy taking care of your own life, family, and soul. Allah is the only One without limits. We as humans should know ours.

When we teach our children to put Allah first, we need to understand that this means He comes before even us.
And while this means they will, *bi'idhnillah*, hold on to their faith throughout their lives, it also means they'll sometimes make life decisions that we neither understand nor agree with.
And if this disturbs us more than the alternative—seeking to control their thoughts and choices—then we need to teach ourselves the same lesson we taught our children.

~

There are no good or bad people in the world, at least not in the absolute sense. There are only sinful people who repent and sinful people who do not repent. It is the presence or absence of repentance that makes a person righteous or corrupt, not the presence or absence of sin.

~

We don't like pain, but it is how our bodies cry out when something is wrong.
We don't like guilt, but it is how our souls cry out when something is wrong.
Don't get frustrated with pain. Tend to the wound.
Don't get frustrated with guilt. Tend to your soul.

A person has not lived life until he dedicates each moment to his preparation for death.

~

I realize that the path I have chosen is a difficult and painful one. But I realize too that the alternative is even more detrimental.

~

It is disheartening to witness a young soul with only a meager thirst for spiritual growth—yet has parents who wish to obliterate even that.

Life.

Priorities.

At this very moment, what is most important to you?
It's whatever you're doing right now.

~

If you are not in the habit of interacting sincerely with the Qur'an every day, as well as praying *Salaah* on time and with concentration, your mind and heart are likely filled with spiritual diseases that you cannot even perceive.
You will imagine that a problem is rooted in one thing, but it's really rooted in another. You will feel completely levelheaded and justified in taking a stance or course of action, but you could be about to ruin your life—and the life of others.
You will think certain people are the source of your annoyance and stress, but your ailing soul is merely crying out for healing, and goes unanswered.
And you may continue on this path of spiritual destruction until evil appears good and good appears evil.
No, reading Qur'an every day and praying on time do not automatically protect you from spiritual diseases and confusion. But these habits definitely make you more likely to *perceive* them.
And therein lies the difference between the destruction of self-deception and the light of repentance.

~

No matter how much knowledge we have, our greatest asset is our sincerity—to ourselves and others. And there is no sincerity without humility, no matter how convinced we are of our spiritual knowledge and good intentions.

Happiness.

When we love someone, we say what they need to know, even if it hurts. That's real love.
Too often we imagine that Satan is behind any hurt, but he's often behind what we call happiness.

~

I'd rather have a difficult, painful road to Paradise than an easy and relaxed, pleasurable path to Hellfire.

~

Gratefulness is a way of life. Remember that. Like faith itself, it doesn't depend on what's happening around you.
It depends on what's happening inside you.
Don't blame your circumstances for your discontentment, frustrations, and spiritual crisis. Blame yourself.
Then ask His help.

Do not let your good deeds be your path to Hellfire.
Ask Allah to remove pride from your heart and scoffing and mocking others from your tongue.

~

No matter what you prefer to call yourself, and no matter what group or school of thought you favor, we'll all be asked the same three questions in the grave. And we'd better have the same answer. So it's best to shed the labels now.
For, certainly, one day they'll be shed for you. And all that will remain are what lies in your heart and how your life reflected that.

~

Pride will not introduce itself to you or warn you that it's about to destroy your life and heart. It will come cloaked in whatever "good cause" is closest to your heart.
If you feel you've been wronged or stripped of something that rightly belongs to you, it will come as your "voice of reason" in demanding what's rightly yours—as it did with Iblis before you.
Be careful. Inflexible conviction in matters that permit, or even demand, flexibility is often a sign that it has settled in your heart.
The only way to protect your heart from pride is to fortify it against itself. And this fortification can only be achieved by constantly turning your heart over to the only One who can protect it from itself.

Lost.

I was afraid I was lost, until I found myself in prayer, begging for direction. Can one who is lost, I thought, be brought before Him, except that He had placed them there?
SubhaanAllah. He had answered my prayer before I'd even thought to make it.

~

Right guidance is not about always knowing what is right.
It is about always remaining on the right path.

~

Your soul is your greatest treasure. Thus, what greater loss is there than losing oneself?

~

Being rightly guided is not about our connection to a specific group or religious teacher. It's about our connection to Allah and following the guidance of His Messenger, peace be upon him.
Those who equate guidance with human beings inevitably equate misguidance with human beings. As such, they often remain blind to their own misguidance because they seek the signs of falsehood outside themselves—instead of in incorrect beliefs and actions, which all humans can fall into, whether layperson or scholar.
The signs of our own misguidance are found through honest self-reflection and prayer, not in our attachment to—or dissociation from—a specific group or teacher. Even the most rightly guided group or teacher cannot protect us from misguidance, and even the most misguided group or teacher cannot block us from guidance.

Tales of the Ancients.

O dear soul, you do not want to be at war with your Lord. Did you not read, "Woe to those who write the Book with their own hands then declare, 'This is from Allah!'" (2:79) We read these *ayaat* as if they are tales of the ancients, of a people who died long ago with no connection to us. Then we close the Book and declare what is *halaal* or *haraam* based on the flimsy desires of our hearts—or on what is most pleasing to the cultures in which we live.

But O dear soul, do you wish to be at war with your Lord? If we are too lazy to pray, we declare that true Islam exists only in the heart.

If we wish to cast aside hijab, we declare that the Qur'an requires only that we "dress modestly."

If we do not want our husbands to marry another wife—or our wives to think we ever would—we declare that polygamy is not allowed in our times.

If we wish to deny the permissible disagreement surrounding music—or any other *ikhtilaaf* issue we refuse to see as such—we declare that anyone who believes it is *haraam* is an extremist,

or that love of Allah and His Book cannot exist in the heart of those believe it is not.

And on and on, we recite the words of men as if they are the Words of Allah.

Meanwhile the angels are recording in our Book of Deeds every word that we utter.

Then we open the Book of Allah and read about those who speak about Allah that of which they have no right or knowledge, and we actually wonder who they are.

Crossroads.

Before crossing any path in life, look both ways—even when you think the path leads only one way.
Things that strike us hardest in life often happen when we least expect—and from places we thought they shouldn't have.

~

Life is about what you make of the choices you make, and what you make of those made for you.

~

Turn your faults and sins into worship and good deeds. How? If you are lazy with your prayers, as soon as you feel the dread, say something like, "O Allah! Make my joy the *Salaah*!" If you love something (or someone) that is forbidden to you, as soon as you feel tempted, say, "O Allah! Make me love what You love and hate what You hate!"
If you feel disconnected from the Qur'an when you read it, turn everything you read into a prayer. So if the passage is about people rejecting the Messengers, you can say, "O Allah! Protect me from being amongst them!" If the passage is about Paradise, say, "O Allah! Make me amongst the inhabitants of Paradise!" If the passage is about Hellfire, say, "O Allah! Protect me from it!"
If you don't even feel like opening the Qur'an, then pray that Allah changes your heart so that you love reading it.
In this way, you turn your faults and sins into worship and good deeds.

Once someone sells you on a label other than Islam, they can sell you on a path other than Islam.
Or at least it's made that much easier.
So my focus is on striving my level best to live up to what my Lord intended for His servants when He called us Muslim.

~

Finding fault in the one reminding you of Allah is nothing new. For prophets and messengers were slandered and opposed as a matter of course. So be careful when you fixate on the faults of the one calling you to repent, more than you do your own sin.
Yes, it is possible the person is arrogant and judgmental; and yes, it is possible they lack wisdom and compassion when they speak.
But it is equally possible that you are merely following in the footsteps of the heedless who came before you—who saw it as their duty to find fault with the messenger, instead of heeding the message itself.

~

Don't become a glorified victim—a person who uses the wrong done by others to justify wronging the self.

Be Quiet.

When two believers who are permissible for each other decide to marry, it is not our right to voice criticism or objection to the matrimony, no matter how "strange" or distasteful the match appears to us. Know that every word you speak publicly, whether with your tongue or on social media, you will be called to account for. And every harm or pain another suffers as a result of your unnecessary speech is written as wrongdoing in your Book of Deeds.

This culture of verbal harassment has caused many Muslim women and people of color to be oppressed and discriminated against worldwide without any real hope for justice or protection. Most oppression does not begin in legislation and politics. It begins in unjust social climates.

So be careful, dear soul, lest you'll be standing on the Day of Judgment opposite men and women you'd never met in your life, but whose lives were brought to ruin due to your loose tongue and hotheaded opinions—and the Master of that Day is demanding you pay for your wrongs.

O child of Adam! Be careful!

Divorce- and polygyny-shaming has no place amongst people who believe in Allah and the Last Day.
But unfortunately, so few Muslims reflect the "good Islam" described by Prophet Muhammad, peace be upon him, when he said, "Part of a person's good Islam is to stay out of matters that do not concern him" (Tirmidhi). And even fewer heed the advice, "Say what is best, or remain silent" (Muslim).

Years ago, two of my closest friends were co-wives, and the open contempt that was shown to them was chilling.
Sisters refused to visit them, saying their friendship was "disgusting" and "fake." Sisters warned me and others to stay away from them, lest our husbands want to marry into polygyny too. I was cautioned to "forbid" my husband from being friends with their husband.
Once, a sister who had no place to stay lived with me for some time, and when the co-wives came to visit, she refused to even come downstairs and give them salaams.
And the list goes on and on.

~

Woe to the ones who confuse their role with God's, thinking their authority over others in this world grants them endless rights that demand perpetual submission to whatever they decree—instead of endless responsibility that demands perpetual repentance for falling short in heeding God's decree. For surely, anyone whose heart is filled with pride—instead of fear—in carrying out their responsibility toward those under them in this world has lost their mind or soul. Or both.
Islam came to free humans from the servitude of men to the servitude of the Creator, yet some who profess belief wish to reinstate the servitude of humans toward man, then claim it is a commandment of God.
Yes, humans have obligations toward those in authority over them. But those in authority have an even greater obligation toward them.
O parents, spouses, and religious teachers, take heed,
take heed!
Before Allah takes your soul.

Music.

My understanding of music has evolved based on my experience, studies, and knowledge. I grew up thinking nothing of music except to avoid obviously bad messages and profane lyrics; then I studied and was taught that music was forbidden and I embraced this view based on being taught that there was complete *ijmaa'* (scholarly and Muslim consensus) from all of the *Sahaabah* and *salaf* with no differing views except those introduced in modern times. When my studies revealed that the claim of historical *ijmaa'* was not completely accurate, I refrained (as I do today) from saying it is prohibited, and instead view music with caution while accepting that it is beyond my ability to determine which side is correct.

Nevertheless, I'm deeply troubled by extremism on both sides: those who say music is "completely okay" and label those who don't listen to it as "extremists," and those who say music is "undoubtedly forbidden" and label those who listen to it as "engaging in clear *haraam*."

I ask Allah to protect me from either extreme, as I fear for my soul if I were to fall into this, as it involves slander of believers while willingly ignoring the Qur'an and Sunnah proofs for both views—not to mention the arrogant assumption that we know what is in someone's mind and heart.

We want others' love and admiration so much that we're willing to sacrifice loyalty to fellow believers—and even Islam itself—to get it.

~

It is a tragic thing to be taught from childhood that you are better than other people. The only thing that this lesson guarantees is that you have a higher likelihood in adulthood of being amongst the worst of people. Because pride destroys goodness like wildfires destroy life—and pride is removed more easily from hearts that never confused it with life itself.

~

Deep.
In the name of compassion and tolerance, we tolerate any number of sins and transgressions when someone is openly disobeying their Lord. But when there is evidence that a person is trying to obey Him, especially when they are also inviting others to Him, we tolerate not even the slightest sin or fault on their part, even if merely a slip of the tongue. Thus, we declare the faults of the "religious" as signs of their hypocrisy, arrogance or cruelty, but rarely of their humanity. It is as if the right to human compassion—or to even being viewed as human at all—is forfeited once you decide to openly obey your Lord.

Trials.

I'm learning to see the good in this trial. Patience and gratefulness are the lessons I am learning from all of this confusion around us: "If you feel it, you should fulfill it. If you want it, you should get it. If you don't like it, cut it off; then mutate the rest with drugs."

Unfortunately, we live in a world that teaches us that our "heart's desire" is both our purpose of existence and our human "right." And if anyone cares enough about us to plead with us, for the sake of our souls, to reconsider this self-harming path, they're suffering from a "phobia" or they're "bigots" lacking compassion.

It is truly heartbreaking and terrifying to wake up each day and realize that, no, this isn't a bad dream. It's the reality of the world—for us and our children—as we draw ever closer to the Day of Judgment.

Seeing how far we can throw ourselves to ruin while genuinely thinking we are in our right minds has taught me to trust God more. It has taught me to be patient through the difficult trials He has given me. It has taught me to not fret so much for what I don't have, and to take more time out for worship and reciting and reflecting on His words.
And when I do this, I find a heart at peace. I find that my true heart's desire is to meet my Lord in a state pleasing to Him. And that is all.

Even if every single day of my life He tests me with passion unrequited, hunger un-satiated, pain unrelieved, and prayers unanswered, there wouldn't be a single part of me that would fret over any of this if I am called back to Him and am told, *"O [you] the one in [complete] rest and satisfaction! Come back to your Lord, well-pleased and well-pleasing unto Him! Enter you, then, among My honored slaves. And enter you My Paradise!"* (Qur'an, 89:27-30).

Our Moral Compass.

As Muslims today, I think the problem we face within ourselves is entitlement and complacency. Allah has given us so much room to live and enjoy our lives as we worship Him that we now think indulging in any and every enjoyment or entertainment is our right. So we've become complacent with listening to, watching, and doing whatever we please.
In this, we've made our personal feelings and opinions the essence of our moral compass, and the ultimate criterion of deciding right and wrong. Yet Allah says, "He sent down the *Furqaan* [the criterion of judgment between right and wrong]" (*Ali'Imraan*, 3:4).

But because our feelings and opinions are our *furqaan* instead of the Qur'an, the Muslims who make the slightest effort at living righteously and speaking about right or wrong based on Allah's Book [the *Furqaan*], we immediately feel in our hearts a sense of distaste or annoyance with them.
This distaste or annoyance is our "moral compass" that is deeply rooted in our sense of self-serving entitlement and religious complacency.
So to protect ourselves against the self-reproaching and self-correcting nature of our souls—which tells us we are wrong for this—we quickly give these Muslims a blameworthy label. And this name-calling (which too violates the principles of Allah's *Furqaan*) calms our hearts, as we tell ourselves, "Islam is balanced. Don't listen to these crazy, narrow-minded people."

But O dear soul, do you not know that your Lord is *As-Saboor*, The Patient One?
So as you return to your life of indulging in any and every entertainment you like, claiming it is your God-given right, *As-Saboor*, the One you speak of, has commissioned His angels to fulfill a duty. And in quiet firmness, they stand at our sides recording all of this in our Book of Deeds, while other angels wait for the signal to seize our souls.
"And they flinch not [from executing] the commands they are given from Allah, but they do [precisely] what they are commanded" (*At-Tahreem*, 66:6).

Then we stand naked, terrified, and vulnerable, the pride and self-satisfaction ripped from our hearts as we emerge in a stupor from our graves. And now, dear soul, *now*...

you meet the One in whose Name you lived in selfish entitlement and spiritual complacency, while calling His believing servants names that He did not give them.

O Allah! We have indeed wronged our souls, so forgive us!

Wherever you find misguidance, you find teachings rooted in the knowledge and life path of someone other than the Prophet, *sallallaahu'laayhi wa sallam*.

~

"You can't be 'just Muslim,'" I was told.
In other words, I apparently had to be a certain *type* of Muslim—by choosing a single group, sect, or school of thought.
"When you go to purchase a car," they told me, "can you purchase 'just a car,' or does it have to be a certain make or model?"
It was one of the most bizarre analogies I'd ever heard.
Firstly, according to whom can I *not* be merely a Muslim? You or Allah?
Furthermore, on what planet does worshipping and obeying God equate with shopping for a car?
My religion is *not* a car, and it isn't for sale. And even if it were, I'm certainly not the one in the driver's seat.

~

Truly, I worry about our spiritual sanity when we begin to claim that a child of Adam who has not been given prophethood is infallible in his religious knowledge, understanding, or teachings. Amongst the earliest Muslims, such a claim was never made about even the most revered of the Prophet's Companions. What then of someone whom neither the Book of Allah nor the tongue of the Prophet, *sallallaahu'alayhi wa sallam*, has even mentioned—and whose abode in the Hereafter is as unknown and uncertain as our own?

> O Allah! Return us to Your religion, and restore 'aql to our hearts and minds!

There is no divine *anything* except what describes Allah Himself. So to speak of anything of creation such that divine attributes are assigned to it—whether a divine human soul, a divine feminine, a divine saint, or a portion of the divine living within us—is the very antithesis of *Tawheed* (Islamic monotheism) and the very essence of *shirk* (paganism).

Shirk.

~

Unconditional obedience is synonymous with "respect" only when it is directed toward God. In any other context, it is the breeding ground for toxic, dysfunctional, and abusive relationships, whether in a marriage, family, or religious group.
Be careful that when you demand "respect" you're not really asking for worship—and that when you show "respect" you're not really putting a human being above God.

~

"For you is your religion, and for me is mine."
Today, I find myself more and more having to say this to professed Muslims. *SubhaanAllah.*

May Allah protect us from misguidance, so that we see truth as truth and follow it, and recognize falsehood as falsehood and stay away from it. And may Allah forgive us our shortcomings, ignorance, and sin in this regard.

Empowerment.

Interesting.
Being "preachy" is only bad when someone is inviting us to celebrate the praises of God and live a life that is pleasing to Him. But being preachy is good when someone is inviting us to celebrate the praises of an "empowering" singer and find life lessons in a context that is displeasing to Him.

~

Do not speak to me about "empowerment" if it doesn't involve living a life of obedience to God.
If you want me to look past obvious moral transgressions to appreciate a "deeper message" in a woman crying about infidelity, then why can't I also look past obvious moral transgressions to appreciate a "deeper message" in why a man cheated in the first place?
Or it is only women who can wrong their souls for a "higher purpose"? And only women whom we should "celebrate" indulging in sin? And only women whose sexuality should be flaunted, God's laws be damned?

By Allah, I have no idea what law book you are following when you ask me to celebrate this.
Or what dictionary you are using when you call this "empowerment."

I find empowerment in only my faith in God—and my hope that I'll be forgiven for the times I lost myself enough to imagine that empowerment and goodness can be found in anything else.

Leadership.

Men, until you know quite distinctly the difference between leading and controlling, you are not ready to lead a family or a community. Men who view their role from the eyes of a controller will inevitably see nearly every individual expression of a woman as modernism and "feminism." Men who view their role from the eyes of a leader will inevitably see nearly every individual expression of a woman as merely a reflection of her humanity in front of God, and he understands that his job is to protect and nurture this healthy emotional and spiritual growth—not stunt it. A controller assumes the worst about those under his care, and a leader assumes the best. As such, a controller will imagine a woman's decision to run a business or go to school as a desire to mix with men and commit sin. A leader will imagine a woman's decision to run a business or go to school as a desire to further her financial and intellectual capabilities while being a benefit to her family and community—unless he has clear evidence otherwise.

Before you apply offensive labels to believing women who recognize that they have their own minds and souls, consider the possibility that there is something wrong with your own.

~

Successful leadership lies in knowing the difference between leading and controlling. Leaders encourage others' growth and improvement—by recognizing and benefiting from others' strengths and abilities; by soliciting and welcoming helpful feedback, even at the risk of hearing what they don't like; and by resolving problems and conflict without becoming part of the problem themselves. Controllers, on the other hand, stunt others' growth and improvement—by micromanaging and becoming frustrated with the weaknesses and "annoying" behavior of others; by ignoring and discouraging helpful feedback, even as they continuously ask for it; and by being completely unable to resolve problems or conflict—because they are often the cause of the problem themselves.

—excerpt of *Pain. From the Journal of Umm Zakiyyah*

Don't die saying that spiritual truth never reached you, when your soul calls out to you every day. You don't have to take a course in theology or have a Muslim friend before you realize you should live and die in submission to God— upon Islam.

~

If anyone tells you that your path to spiritual salvation lies anywhere outside the clear, simple principles of the Quran and prophetic teachings, then know they are inviting you to a faith other than Islam, and a path other than Paradise.

~

Interesting how many Muslims consider it "fatwa shopping" to follow an Islamic opinion they personally disagree with. But it's "respecting scholars" or "following the evidences" when it's an opinion they agree with. And when they discuss an issue by saying, "I believe such and such", it's just expressing their agreement with a permissible scholarly view, but when someone they disagree with says, "I believe such and such" regarding a permissible scholarly view, the person is accused of making up their own rulings and disregarding evidences.
May Allah guide us.

Lonely.

This is a lonely journey, I cannot lie.
Holding on to your faith, I mean.
It's not supposed to be. But it is.
It sometimes feels as if making the decision to practice Islam openly is a contractual agreement between you and the rest of the world, saying that it's completely okay for them to make your life miserable—emotionally, psychologically and practically. That it's completely okay for them to follow and announce your faults. That it's completely okay for them to blame you for everything that's gone wrong in the name of God and religion. That it's completely okay for them to harass, abuse, and bully you—while you aren't allowed to have even *unspoken* beliefs that they find offensive.
And that it's completely okay for those closest to you—whether through the bond of faith, friendship, or blood—to watch you suffer and say you deserved it.
Because you had the audacity to make others uncomfortable by holding on to your faith at all.

~

What have we come to when we seek to shield our scholars and leaders from our true feelings and frustrations under the guise of "respect"? What then is the role of a scholar or leader if not to tend to the people's concerns?
And do you know *anyone* who would count as "respect" a trusted friend or loved one hiding their true feelings while smiling to your face, speaking only words of reverence and praise? Yet they remain silent—even when asked—about what really weighs on their mind and heart.

~

Don't ever let an abuser make your hurt and concerns about your religious obligation to them. Inciting guilt is the only ammunition they have since they refuse to face themselves.

Emotional abusers are masters at turning their sins into your wrongs. Your every complaint, disagreement, or expression of concern is now about you not showing them enough love, compassion, or respect. And as soon as they fear that others will see their wrongdoing for what it is, they play victim and accuse you of hurting them in some way.

These abusers can be family members, friends, or religious teachers—and they can be sociopolitical activists seeking to sell a sinful lifestyle to the world while blocking even the chance at opposition.

~

For centuries, society has sought to trivialize, disrespect, and silence women, often seeking to erase their significance from the pages of history. And today, we are seeing one of the greatest injustices ever inflicted upon them in the era of humankind: the outright denial of their very existence.

When we had nothing, we at least had our God-given identity, announced to the world upon birth. No, it wasn't much, but we embraced it and gave sweat and blood—and sometimes even our lives—as we demanded respect and recognition based upon this divine gift.

And now, we are being denied even that.

Now, womanhood is merely a feeling.

Now, womanhood is merely a hormone produced in a lab.

Now, womanhood can be sucked up and packed into a syringe.

Now, womanhood can be sent through a needle into the veins of a man.

Now, womanhood can be a public spectacle of the mentally ill playing dress-up in our bodies and clothes.

By God, I feel sick—to my stomach and soul.

I have never felt so disrespected in my life.

Disrespected.

Enough.

I can't do it anymore. I *won't* do it anymore.
I will no longer tiptoe around my deepest emotions, whether in happiness or anger. I will no longer tolerate people in my personal space telling me I have a "responsibility" to shun worldly expressions of happiness, or human expressions of offense and anger.
If I want to laugh, dance, or sing, I will do it. If I want to defend myself, my religion, or my brothers and sisters in faith, I will do it, *bi'idhnillaah*. And I couldn't care less if the feelings of an open aggressor or fake victim are hurt.

These people have shamelessly assaulted me, my religion, and my loved ones for far too long, while we run to and fro like pandering slaves, frantically calling for soft words of kindness and compassion to protect their oh-so-tender feelings. Meanwhile, the very backs and hearts of believers are broken relentlessly, and unapologetically so, at their tongues and hands.

So no, I can't do it anymore. I *won't* do it anymore. I refuse.

~

If you're not applying the principles of compassion to yourself at the very moment you're insisting on it from someone else, it really is unfair to mention compassion at all. Like sincerity and doing things "for the sake of Allah," our Lord teaches us these concepts as a self-check—a means to better ourselves and purify our own souls—not as a means to find fault in someone else.
Moreover, it really is impossible to look at someone's outward behavior and speech and know what is going on in their heart. However, we are self-centered people—may Allah guide us and forgive us—because we actually believe our feelings, whether in hurt or happiness, are valid measures of good or evil in someone else.
But Allah is taking account of it all, so I pray we are humble and wise enough to self reflect and self correct before we stand before the One from whom no good or evil is hidden, even when we were able to hide it from ourselves.

Emotionalism.

Beware of emotionalism. It is like a cheating spouse. Faithful to nothing except what excites it at the moment. Follow it and you'll find yourself constantly off balance, furious, and confused, even if you've no idea why.
Principles and morality are more dependable.
They remain faithful, no matter what excitement is happening in the world.
So choose principles and morality over emotionalism.
They are the cornerstones of faith.

~

Emotionalism turns spirituality into narcissism, wherein our feelings are the strongest criterion of right and wrong—and these feelings become the lens through which we interpret divine scripture.
However, in authentic spirituality, divine scripture is the strongest criterion of right and wrong—and God's teachings becomes the lens through which we understand our feelings.

Fear.

From the Journal of Umm Zakiyyah

Test or Punishment.

"How do I know if it's a test or a punishment?"
This is a question I wondered about for years, and every chance I got, I asked an Islamic teacher or read whatever I could on the issue. Till today, the answer that stays with me is this: You don't.

Ultimately, only Allah knows why He's putting believers through certain trials. Also, a test and a punishment are not mutually exclusive. Both could be happening at once.

All of life is a test for the human being, so everything we experience is meant to direct us back to our purpose: worshipping and serving our Creator. Whether we are experiencing ease or hardship, enjoying the worldly fruit of honest hard work, or suffering the bitter consequences of arrogantly disobeying Allah; we have in each circumstance the opportunity to seek Allah's pleasure, beg His forgiveness, and attain Paradise when we die.

In other words, even if the worst is true—we're being punished for our sins—this in itself isn't "the end of the world." Often, believers experience pain, trials, and punishment on earth so that they are spared from torment for their sins in the Hereafter.

And if the worldly trial—or punishment—is encouraging us to turn to Allah, repent, and improve our spiritual lives; what practical benefit do we gain from obsessing over whether or not Allah is angry with us?

Unless we are arrogantly seeking to continue disobeying Allah and need a serious reality check, fixating on this question can become a distraction from spiritual growth itself.

No matter what is or is not happening in our life (and why), we should be worshipping Allah and seeking His guidance and forgiveness anyway.

And would—or should—knowing whether you are facing a trial or a punishment change this noble focus for you?

Distractions.

If you can find no other criticism of someone than the label "judgmental," then keep quiet until you can find a more mature, specific point of disagreement.
If you cannot, then reflect on the possibility that the problem is within you.

~

When you can't attack the argument, attack the person.
I'm amazed at how widespread this tactic is in otherwise mature conversations today.

Personally, I feel disappointed whenever I hear terms like "judgmental" or "arrogant" issued in a discussion about religion and principles of right and wrong. It inevitably distracts from the issue at hand and thwarts any possibility of coming to a solution.

It is beyond me what someone's personal mindset or heart issue has to do with whether or not we should pray five times a day, wear hijab, or follow Allah's laws on sexuality. Unless someone is engaged in obvious wronging or harming others, this sort of name-calling says more about our own mindset and heart issues than it does about the person we're criticizing.

When the terms are aimed at me, I often remind people, "I'm not perfect, and I would never claim that my heart is 100% pure. But can you please tell me what my personal faults have to do with the obligation of all of us to obey Allah?"

Perception.

I claim no perfection in conveying the truth.
However, I encourage you to sincerely reflect on the fact that your reactions and opinions do not reflect reality.
They reflect only your personal feelings, emotions, and opinions. Thus, to use terms like "judgmental attitude" indicate a very faulty path in communication and perception, as they imply that your internal world reflects the reality of the world around you.

And how do you decide whose feelings and emotions matter more, yours or mine? Or are *all* of our feelings valid? If so, then exactly what does "judgmental attitude" mean to you? But more importantly, what does it mean to ALLAH?

So I caution you to be very careful with your words, especially when they are casting wide nets of judgments on someone for no crime other than conveying the truth of Islam in a way *you* don't like.

Except in cases of obvious verbal abuse and harm, feelings of discouragement or being judged are merely signs of internal personal struggles and emotionalism, nothing more.
And we all have internal personal struggles and emotionalism, as this is a trait of being human.

Yes, it is helpful to share our personal struggles and emotionalism from time to time, as this allows us to be more aware and sensitive to those around us.

However, the problem is when we process our personal struggles and emotions as an external problem in someone else (i.e. judgmental attitude) instead of an internal human experience that reflects only ourselves.

May Allah guide us and help us such that we react to reminders about our souls with the inspiration to correct ourselves instead of the one conveying the reminder.

—UZ to a commenter on "I'm Muslim and Don't Pray. What Should I Do?"

Fear of People.

"I don't care what people think!" many of us boast.
But is that really true?
If it is, why then do we keep saying, "Don't judge"?
The popularity and earnestness of this statement alone means we actually care a great deal about what people think. Otherwise, their judgment (or lack thereof) wouldn't matter to us, and we certainly wouldn't feel the need to keep exclaiming, "Don't judge!"

~

Be honest with yourself.
What is making you hesitate in taking that step you *know* you need for spiritual improvement?
What is it that you're *really* scared of?

I know for myself, when I've stayed frozen in a state I knew wasn't good for me, it was due to some worldly fear of the unknown and to how the people I loved and valued would treat me once I changed. This is no small matter.
Even the Prophet (peace be upon him) needed the intervention of God Himself to offer comfort and reassurance amidst the harsh treatment and judgment of others.
Though he certainly didn't let their speech and behavior turn him away from his spiritual duty, he did in fact care what they thought—as any sensitive and gentle soul would.
Why then do we imagine we're immune to this human struggle?

Today, most people who learn the truth of Islam and hesitate to accept it for themselves have very real fears about a drastic life change, and about facing the thoughts and judgments of those who matter to them most.
But what comfort and advice can we offer them if we're not even being honest with ourselves about the fears and hesitations for improvement—due to fear of people—that we have in our own lives?

Guardians.

Adjectives are guardians of conscience.
If we can affix a praiseworthy adjective to something we want or love, it gives us a clear conscience, even if we are in sin.
If we can affix a blameworthy adjective to something (or someone) we despise or look down upon, it gives us a clear conscience, even if we are the wrong or misguided one.
But the adjective frees us, for it is our guardian.
It hides us from ourselves.

~

It really is okay to keep your mouth shut, your mind open, and your heart pure.
Here's a three-word shortcut that can help you:
mind your business.

~

The "self" is not in the skin or the blood. It is in the soul.
So any "self pride" and "self preservation" rooted in skin color or ethnicity alone is just a euphemism for arrogance, racism, and wrongdoing—to the self and others.

Emotional Manipulation.

Please don't pull the victim card in a mature discussion, where as soon as it's clear you might not "win" the argument (whatever that means), you accuse the person of being mean to you. Either speak like grown people—with an existence outside your hurt feelings—or stay out of the conversation.

~

Like our overuse of "for the sake of Allah," when we speak about compassion and wisdom, it's almost always in the context of what we insist on from *someone else*.
Yet in our faith, these concepts are to be applied to ourselves. That we use them to criticize, shame, and guilt others to do what we think they should, should tell us that we don't *really* want others' sincerity, compassion, and wisdom.
We just want to move through life with only *our* needs met, our feelings protected, and our opinions heard, as if no one else's exist.
Then when we don't get our way, we accuse people of being insincere or arrogant, and of lacking compassion.
This in itself should give us a glimpse into why unless someone's feeding our ego and agreeing with us, our hearts almost never perceive these qualities in someone else—because we've yet to truly experience them within ourselves.

~

There *is* such a thing as simply having hurt feelings and nothing more. We don't have to turn every pain or frustration into someone else's fault.

Masquerade.

Those who believe God's teachings are a source of evil on earth are testifying to the source of evil in their own hearts. This is because good and evil are rooted in the human's internal world before they are manifested in humans' external world.

A person sincerely striving for purity in the heart does not have the ability to read the words of God and use them for spreading corruption on earth. This is because a person can only spend from what he has, and a man's words and actions are the currency through which he negotiates his dealings on earth.

And the minimal reflection of a heart's good currency is a belief in God and submission to Him, and the most obvious reflection of a heart's evil currency is the denial of God and rejecting His teachings.

~

I think, in the quiet of the night, at certain moments, you see your depraved reflection before you, and you feel repulsed. But instead of facing the corruption of your soul, you blame God and religion for making you feel guilty about yourself.
So no, there's nothing more I can say to you.
You refuse to hear even yourself.
   —a note to the anti-religious masquerading as the "do gooder"

~

If biology doesn't determine gender, then why get surgeries and take hormones to match the biology of the gender you prefer? You could simply say you're male or female and remain exactly as you are.

But you don't, because you know very well that biology *does* determine gender. And our biology comes from none other than the Creator.

He says, "And the male is not like the female" (Qur'an, 3:36). And I believe Him.

Of the greatest injustices is to teach men and women that they are equal. It would be better for them both to be told the truth. That no two souls are equal.
And that it is justice—not equality—that the Creator guarantees to each soul at birth.

~

Men and women are equal in their accountability for their souls in front of Allah. After that, I'm not sure we're being fully honest when we claim they are "equal" as far as modern definitions go.
The man is the leader of the home, masjid, and society, and I have no problem with that.
In fact, I find it quite off-putting for men to deny their roles as leaders in the name of avoiding patriarchy and "empowering women." No thank you.
I've never met a woman who's impressed with an emasculated man.
Yes, we want to feel empowered, but not at the expense of your manhood. It's sufficient for you to be secure enough with yourself such that you don't feel threatened by our intelligence, talents, and abilities.
And that you rather *encourage* these—as we'll do for you.

~

Upon marriage, you must learn to live with another person, which is amongst the most difficult trials on earth.
For what could be more trying than learning to live with yourself?

Just because we don't like or feel comfortable with something doesn't mean it's "disliked" or forbidden in the religion.
When we advise people not to follow their desires, remember that goes both ways: We shouldn't follow *our* desires—in seeking to find the *haraam* in other people's.

~

Here's the problem.
Many of us want to believe that anything that upsets us automatically upsets the Creator. So our thinking effectively becomes inflexible divine law, and we turn to the Qur'an and Sunnah only to obtain "*daleel*" for what we already believe. Then we rage against "vices" like divorce, polygamy, and even a different point of view on a matter of permissible disagreement.
Yet we manage to convince ourselves that it is Islam we're insisting everyone follow, while in reality we are only insisting that everyone follow us.

~

Following the faults of others isn't manifested only in sinful behavior like gossiping and backbiting.
It is also manifested in ostensibly righteous behavior like advising others and giving *naseehah*—especially when our critiques are constant and unsolicited.
Too often our "advice" is rooted more in our own opinions, frustrations, and emotions than in anything we can be fully certain is the only view in the Qur'an and Sunnah.
One sign that we are following the faults of others is when our faith offers another view of what we disagree with, but we criticize others as if they are violating a fundamental, inflexible part of Islam.

Gratification.

Instant gratification can be an addiction.
Beware of it affecting your faith and worship.
Everything good and beneficial doesn't always feel good right away. Sometimes it never feels good right away.
But we don't do what is right and necessary because it feels good. We do what is right and necessary because it is right and necessary.

~

I find the advice to "fill the heart with love of Allah before praying (or doing good)" is one of the most impossible and stressful pieces of advice I've ever heard. Personally, hearing this only makes me feel worse, like I'm a bad Muslim since I don't feel that all the time, and certainly not every time it's time to pray.
But knowing that Allah doesn't require me to be perfect when I stand in front of Him in *Salaah* is a much more merciful perspective. And, *alhamdulillaah*, it also happens to be the true, Islamic perspective.
So that's what I prefer to hold on to, the merciful truth, instead of an impossible, stressful standard I could never uphold.

May Allah forgive us and guide us upon His religion and make our words and lives inspiration to others.

—UZ to a commenter on "I'm Muslim and Don't Pray. What Should I Do?"

Tyrannical Religion.

Interesting.

It's "oppressive" for religious people to force their beliefs on others, but it's perfectly fine—and good and necessary even—for non-religious people to force *their* beliefs on others.

So it's a "victory" for laws to be passed forcing religious people to commit sin at work, so long as the action can be labeled an "obligation" or "duty" on the job.

But it's "unjust" for laws to be passed to force non-religious people to do what they personally *feel* shouldn't be an obligation or duty—according to God or anyone else—even if it is merely accommodating a religious person on the job.

Thus, injustice is only evil if God's name is involved.

But if the label is "secular," the same act of wrongdoing is labeled "freedom" or "human rights."

But here's the truth: modern secularism is just another type of tyrannical religion.

~

By definition, implementing "laws" means forcing a specific belief system on others irrespective of their personal or moral objections to the rules. So it's hypocritical to claim you think it's wrong for people to force their belief system on others, yet you champion a society based on laws.

So unless you believe anarchy is the only system of justice on earth, please stop lying to yourself and others saying you stand against people being forced to follow others' beliefs. Anyone who believes in a legal system believes in *some* beliefs being forced. It's just a matter of *which* beliefs you think should be law.

~

Topics are only secular when the spiritual element is forcibly removed from them. There is nothing on this earth that doesn't belong to the Creator.

Fragile Egos.

I don't want to be the person whom people avoid due to the stress I evoke.

I don't want to be the one whom my friends appease because even when I'm wrong and hurting others, I'm too insecure to handle anything but praise, smiles and support.

I don't want to be the parent whose children hold their breath in my presence, afraid to show even the slightest sign of having a thought or mind of their own.

I don't want to be the teacher who makes my students cringe because they have no idea what hell I'll unleash on them that day.

I don't want to be the leader with an ego so fragile that the slightest bump sends it crashing to the ground, shattered and broken, and then I blame the person for not knowing how untouchable, superior and invaluable I was.

And I don't want to be the person who blames others because holding others accountable for the ailing of my soul is so much easier and less painful than facing myself.

Prayer.

From the Journal of Umm Zakiyyah

O dear soul who rushes through Prayer,
Is there somewhere you absolutely *must* go…
Other than Jannah?

~

How can you be so excited about something that you barely concentrate in Prayer or you rush through it? Yet you're standing before the One who granted you that good, and the only thing a proper prayer could change is that the good is increased for you.

~

A person who has *khushoo'* in *Salaah* can house no more than a grain of pride in his heart. Because no more than that can grow in the time span between two prayers.

Khushoo'.

Open your eyes and stand before Allah under the cover of darkness so that He will open your eyes and guide you under the light of day.

~

I fear if my body does not awaken at night to pray, my heart will remain asleep during the day.

~

I cannot feel comfortable spending the entire night wrapped up in my blanket when I know that I spent the entire day wrapped up in myself.

Submission.

Pray with your heart, not with your body.
And you will find your limbs follow in submission,
as they have no other choice.

~

Let your prayer emanate from your heart,
and your body will reflect that Light.

~

As you pray, let your heart lead, and your body will follow.
Do not let your body lead,
expecting your heart to follow.

Sincerity.

In prayer, I often find my heart struggling to follow the movement of my limbs, as if searching in the motion for some semblance of the soul's sincerity.
That is how I know in all these years that I've prayed,
it is rare that I've actually prayed.

~

A person has not tasted the sweetness of faith until they find peace and relaxation in Prayer.

Faith.

There is within our hearts no more than a grain of faith if we do not find tranquility and solace in Prayer.

~

Deficiency in faith has its symptoms in one's deficiency in Prayer.

~

How can I say I believe in Allah and the Hereafter when I stand before Allah five times each day while my heart and mind are preoccupied with the affairs of this world?

A Contradictory Prayer.

When I was at my lowest, I prayed a "contradictory prayer," one that was infused with so much goodness that it contradicted nearly everything I felt and believed about myself at the time.

If I felt dread or laziness at the time for prayer, I prayed, "O Allah, make my joy the *Salaah*!"

If I could not wrap my heart or mind around something I knew I should do, I prayed, "O Allah, increase me in knowledge and understanding, and make me love what You love."

Some might call it the prayer of a hypocrite, because my words were so far from my actions.

But even so, Allah hears and answers even the supplication of one who struggles with sincerity and steadfastness upon what is right—so long as they have faith in the One who removes all diseases of the heart.

So have faith, dear soul, and turn to your Lord for help. You cannot heal your own heart, and you cannot guide yourself upon the right path.

Servitude.

There is but one form of slavery that raises a person's honor and status while endowing them with strength of character and the illumination of knowledge and wisdom—servitude toward the Creator.

~

Islam is not a philosophy and thus cannot be mastered through classes and books. It is not a scientific discipline in which you can become a "specialist" due to rigorous study. And it is not an academic subject in which a teacher can declare that you passed or failed.
Islam is life. And you can't get a degree or a certificate in "life."
Yes, you can study *about* life.
But in the end, you still have to live it.
And you can only pray to God—in fear and hope—that you're getting it right.

~

Allah will take care of you as long as you take care of yourself—and He'll even help you take care of yourself.

It is true that energy doesn't lie.
But let's not forget that the strongest energy that surrounds us is our own. Thus, sometimes the negative vibes we perceive from others are actually coming from ourselves. When we are not in the habit of establishing the *Salaah* and praying with *khushoo'*, of sincerely supplicating to Allah in *du'aa* and repentance, and of reading and humbly reflecting on the Qur'an every day of our lives, our outlook on the world around us becomes negative and bleak.

And no matter how hard we try, we could never accurately process what is going on with someone else, as we haven't even made minimal effort in understanding what is going on within ourselves.

So before you "trust your gut" in making negative assumptions about someone else, sincerely reflect on the lens through which your troubled soul is seeing the world.

Troubled Souls.

If you want to change something with your hands, the best place to start is raising them in prayer.

~

There are some questions only you can answer.
So perhaps that's why your heart remains doubtful and uncertain after searching for the answer outside yourself.

Change.

There is no success—of any kind—without faith and Prayer.
Call what you have whatever you want, but without these,
it is not success.

~

Death.
It's coming whether you're ready or not.
You might as well be ready.

Success.

Giving Up.

When we give up, we think it's because we're tired of standing before Allah as a sinner.
But we're really tired of standing before Allah as a repentant. Because when you give up, you don't give up sin. You give up repenting.
But either way, you're in front of Allah.

This is perhaps why not praying or supplicating is equated with arrogance in front of Allah. There really is no other explanation for becoming so frustrated with being humble before your Lord that you refuse to ever do it again.

~

"And your Lord says, 'Call on Me, I will answer your [prayer]. But those who are too arrogant to worship Me will surely find themselves in Hell, in humiliation.'"
—Qur'an (*Ghaafir*, 40:60)

"Say, O My slaves who have wronged their souls! Despair not of the mercy of Allah.
Verily, Allah forgives all sins.
Truly, He is Oft-Forgiving, Most Merciful."
—Qur'an (*Az-Zumar*, 39:53)

Patience.

From the Journal of Umm Zakiyyah

Windows.

There is a saying, "The eyes are a window to the soul." I always thought of it as a person seeing into the soul of another by merely looking at him. But now I think it is a person seeing into their own soul by reflecting on what their eyes see in others.

~

I look forward to the day when we search for good to support in people, instead of for the evil to forbid and condemn.

~

Terrifying.
Two people destined for Hellfire can be arguing with each other, and each is 100% correct in pointing out the faults and sins of the other. But they throw themselves to ruin because they never took the time to honestly assess the fault and sin within themselves.

We all struggle with laziness, weak will power, despair, and loss of faith. But none of these are mutually exclusive to arrogance, ignorance, or sin entering our hearts or lives—even if we don't perceive what is happening.

In other words, we can feel lazy, weak, and despondent and still be arrogant, ignorant, and sinful. Because arrogance, ignorance, and sin are not *feelings*.
And they are not opinions regarding what is happening to us. They are realities known to Allah, even if they are unknown to us.

It is very rare that a human being will *feel* arrogant.
It is also very rare that humans will feel as sinful as they really are, even when they know they're sinful.
Even psychologists describe humans as "rationalizing beings" more than "rational beings" because we tend more toward self-justification than self-honesty.

We are all struggling with similar trials of the heart. But we should never think our feelings perceive everything that is going on. So arrogance can certainly be present in our hearts, even if we have no idea it's there.

Prophet Muhammad, *sallallaahu'alayhi wa sallam*, described *kibr* (arrogance) as two things: looking down upon people and rejecting the truth.
We tend to think of only the first part of the definition, but it's rare that we realize that turning away from the truth (i.e. the reality and enormity of our sins) is also a part of *kibr* in front of Allah.

> *May Allah forgive us, have mercy on us, and remove* kibr *from our hearts. And may He allow us to enter Paradise even though we could never deserve it.*

∼

Allah relieves us from the burden of perception through the obligation of submission.

Activism.

When your activism is rooted in soul-work, no topic is trivial. So yes, people are still talking about *that*—because it's about Allah, not you.

~

Don't be the one who speaks up only to tell others to shut up—under the guise of telling them to get their priorities straight. Yes, priorities are important, but ours should never include disregarding someone else's. You are not Allah. Therefore, you don't know what He wants most from them right now.

Dismissing others' concerns by telling them what they should be concerned about isn't activism. It's narcissism. We will never have a loving, united ummah until we learn to listen with our hearts—even to issues that we don't understand or think are important.

That it matters to someone you love should be enough to make it matter to you—that is, if you truly love them, as all believers should.

But if the topic *really* doesn't matter to you, then keep quiet and focus on what does. By speaking up and saying that someone's concern doesn't matter is really just another way of saying that *they* don't matter. And all souls matter to Allah. Thus, they should matter to you—if you have your priorities straight.

Shaming.

Share, don't shame.
If there's anything I learned in all my travels and being in the company of the religious, the political, and the activist, it is this. Those who respected people most benefited people most.
Unless your only goal is to show how superior you are to everyone else, then there really is no point in shaming and humiliating people into taking a certain course of action or following a certain point of view.
Conveying the actual, real life benefits of a particular approach or stance is more than sufficient—as opposed to calling people sinful, lazy, or ignorant if they don't do what you think they should.

In the short term, emotional manipulation and name-calling can certainly inspire people to follow a certain religious point of view, to vote in a certain election, or to become more "racially conscious." But in the long-term, these tactics don't effect lasting change.
They effect lasting harm.
Shaming people has three likely results:
1. unhealthy dependency upon the one inciting shame
2. continuing the cycle of emotional manipulation or abuse
3. recognizing the manipulation and thus distancing oneself from the manipulator

In *none* of these is anyone actually meaningfully changed in their religion, politics, or activism.
So try sharing beneficial information instead of shaming innocent people—if paving the road to a better world is truly your goal.

Truth.

Too often when we hurt someone with our words, we say, "The truth hurts."
But perhaps, it's not the truth that hurt them. We did.

~

Whatever you do, don't forget who you are, where you came from, and Who created you—and that purifying the heart and soul is never done.

~

When seeking to implement the prophetic instruction, "Do not become angry," we need to understand that there are different types of anger, and there are different levels of anger.

What we are being cautioned against is anger that harms the self and others. What we are *not* being cautioned against is the type of anger that a human naturally feels—and expresses—in the face of wrongdoing and oppression, or in the process of healing emotional wounds after suffering years of abuse.

Prison.

Those who seek to overcome their desires by asking others to adjust themselves—in clothing, behavior, or speech—have yet to learn the existence of their human heart and the use of their limbs.
For it is only in these two places that desires are overcome.

~

Oh, what corrupt soul would keep another captive without their consent? And what manipulative soul would torment another, proclaiming it is "love" that renders him unable to set the prisoner free? Yet he remains heartless as she cries in distress for freedom beyond the rusted bars of a relationship that suffocates her to the very core.
Know, dear men, that women have rights to their own souls, and their own lives. They are not bound to you as captives for life.
And know, dear women, that this same cry for freedom—the one that renders your throat dry from agony in search of relief—it emanates from the souls of men too.
So do not torment them with emotional manipulation and guilt trips when they desire life beyond your prison bars.
Demand of yourself what you demand of men.
Set them free.

~

When your interactions with your children or husband or wife focus more on demanding your rights than on cultivating a healthy, emotionally safe relationship,
then the problem is much more serious than who is right or who is wrong.
Something much deeper and more destructive is happening.
In your soul.
Or in the soul of your relationship.

Sometimes the best way to change something with your tongue is to stop talking—because too often our speech causes more problems than those we intend to solve with our words.

~

Respect and agreement are not synonyms.
Both parents and Islamic teachers would do well to reflect on this basic truth.

~

If someone starts a fire, the priority is to put out the fire and save lives, not to protect their wounded pride because they didn't mean to start it.
—on speaking publicly on an issue vs. advising someone privately

Problems.

It's true that some things are easier said than done.
But it's also true that some things are easier done than said.
Because there are simply some things for which words and explanations can do no justice.

~

Please don't put the burden of your soul on others, no matter how much you admire or benefit from them—and no one should put the burden of their soul on you.
"Every soul carries the load of none but itself, and no bearer of burdens can bear the burden of another" (*Al-An'aam*, 6:164).
Islamic sisterhood and brotherhood is a two-way street.
I help you, and you help me. But casting blame does not belong on this path.
So don't blame someone for your weak faith or sins.
We *influence* each other, but we do not carry the burden of each other's souls. Let's not forget that.

~

Letting go and moving on are not the same as burning bridges.
Sometimes a bridge grows stronger only after you step off.

Distractions.

What are the "distractions of this world"?
Often in the name of "eradicating evil," we make lists of them—watching TV, reading novels, playing games, singing songs, and so on.
But let us be careful.
What is a distraction for one person may not be a distraction for someone else—because what distracts you from the right path might not distract them, and vice versa.
And let's not forget that worrying about what other people should and shouldn't be doing is itself a "distraction of this world."
So focus on your own soul. And when it comes to others, focus on calling to Allah. If someone answers that call, then any mistake, sin, or "distraction" they fall into can and, *bi'idhnillah*, will be forgiven.
That's Allah's promise to the believers.
So in our zeal to do good, let's not get distracted from this simple point.

~

Want to make history? You already have.
A book is being written about you right now:
your Book of Deeds.

"And We have fastened every man's deeds to his neck, and on the Day of Resurrection, We shall bring out for him a book which he will find wide open. (It will be said to him): "Read your book. You yourself are sufficient as a reckoner against you this Day."
—Qur'an (*Al-Israa*, 17:13-14)

Disappointment.

I think disappointment in people is a mercy from God.
It's a reminder that we've lost focus and raised creation above the status that God has written for them.
And in the process, we forgot where real greatness comes from—God alone.

~

When we admire or benefit greatly from someone, they often hold a special place in our hearts and a lofty place in our minds. In this, we unwittingly ascribe to them high standards that they, naturally, know nothing about. And when they err or sin, like all children of Adam do, we become upset and disappointed, and we sometimes feel betrayed.
If they were a loved one like a spouse, parent, or favored child, our relationship is often broken or tense as a result.
If they were an admired religious teacher or scholar, we often abandon them for their "hypocrisy" in standards they never claimed.
Shukr—gratefulness. This is what we lack when we fall into this. All good comes from Allah.
So be grateful for the good He has placed in those who are blessings in your life. But do not raise them to a level that Allah has not written for any of His slaves.
The most any of us can hope for is Allah's mercy, so when someone you admire or benefit greatly from falls into error or sin, do not feel disappointed or betrayed. Rather feel grateful that you now can give back to them—by raising your hands in supplication and asking Allah to have mercy on them.

Unity.

Is your community, group, and "clique" better than the assembly of believers in Paradise? Why then do you refuse to welcome into your hearts and circles those whom Allah welcomes into His Paradise? Meanwhile the Qur'an and Sunnah are unequivocally clear that Paradise is for *anyone* who submits to Allah alone and does not fall into *shirk*. Yet our hearts and circles have gatekeepers that forbid entry to these beloved servants. And why?
Because they committed the "unforgivable sin" of not worshipping *us* alone—even as they've committed no unforgivable sin in front of Allah?

It doesn't matter whether you believe music is permissible or *haraam*, whether you believe everyone should or shouldn't vote in elections, whether someone loves your sheikh or *madh-hab* as much as you do, whether someone is down for "the cause" as much you say they should be, or even whether they are apparently sinful or righteous.
They are your brother and sister in Islam by the commandment of Allah. He says, "The believers are but a single brotherhood…" (49:10).
Thus, if you create unnecessary division between yourself and other believers based on your personal views, convictions, and pride—no matter how convinced you are that you are right—then you are guilty of serious wrongdoing.
So I caution you, dear soul, fear Allah.

That Allah promises the opportunity of forgiveness for *all* sins except *shirk* in exchange for our belief in Him should be sufficient evidence that a Muslim need not be perfect in their beliefs and practice before we unite with them.
Our sisterhood and brotherhood is not merely a "good idea" or a "make a wish" project that we talk about as if we're completely helpless in attaining it. It's a spiritual obligation that Allah has placed on every believing child of Adam until the Day of Judgment.
And the only question is: Are you humbly fulfilling this obligation, or are you arrogantly dismissing it?

When we see someone struggling in their faith or who has let go of Islam completely, some of us say, "Well, if they had true faith, they'd never let go of the religion. Allah makes Muslims, not me."
Why do we speak like this? Because our words are true?
Or because we don't want to hold the mirror in front of our faces and admit the hand we played in this—and that we ourselves could very well end up the same?
So instead of turning up our noses and scoffing at them, let's say, "If that were me, what would I want someone to do for me?"
And whatever the answer is, do that.

~

If you're going to move forward in life, you have to embrace the struggle and hurt like you embrace the blessings and happiness. No, I don't mean you rejoice during struggles and hardship, and I don't mean you should like to hurt.
But embrace the full spectrum of what life means.
And when things get hard, bear the difficulty patiently and seek the lesson in it—and that better part of yourself.

When Allah grants you beneficial knowledge, whether religious or otherwise, your duty is to share with others what they should know, not to shame His servants for not knowing.

~

The path of seeking knowledge, what is it?
Is it books? Is it classes? Is it an Islamic university?
I think it is a life of faith, a life of prayer, and a life of reading the Qur'an and acting on it.
It is striving to be better than you were the day before.
It is never giving up your fight against the self.
It is charity, it is smiling at a stranger, and it is being humble and compassionate to others.
That's the path of knowledge that I hope to seek—because it is Paradise that I hope to reach.

~

If your acquisition of religious knowledge has convinced you that the people owe you instead of the other way around, then know that you have not acquired knowledge.
You have acquired pride and self-deception.

In spiritual matters, knowledge alone is not true knowledge. Otherwise Iblis would be amongst the greatest of Islamic scholars. It is not without reason that Allah describes scholars as those who fear Him (35:28).
Check your heart. It is where true knowledge lies.

Seeking Knowledge.

In adversity—facing extreme difficulty—is a humbling spiritual beauty, wherein the heart finally calms in submission to a Greater plan at work, even as the mind remains in unrest and the eyes fill with tears.

~

Of the highest levels of patience is for the body to endure severe pain or the heart to suffer tremendous agony, yet the soul finds peace in the knowledge of its Lord.

Endurance.

Prosperity.

Don't focus on staying motivated.
Focus on staying active.
It is through staying active that we prosper.
Because let's face it: Every time we wake up and see that it's time for prayer, whether for *Tahajjud* or *Fajr*, we're not always happy or "motivated" to get out of bed and pray.
So I tell myself, *No problem. Just get up anyway.*
Or...
No problem, just give charity anyway
No problem, just [do that good deed, whatever it is] anyway...
And Allah will take care of the rest.

Religion.

From the Journal of Umm Zakiyyah

Representing Islam.

Islam doesn't need a makeover to become more appealing to people. People's hearts need a makeover so that Islam becomes more appealing to them.

Yet we as Muslims defend so much in the name of "representing Islam"—as if this perfect religion needs our insecurity and apologetics to "look better" in the eyes of people, people whom *we* want to impress.

But Islam doesn't need people. People need Islam.

And if our "representation" does not reflect the dignity and honor of Islam itself, it is not truly a representation of this faith, no matter how much we want to convince ourselves otherwise.

"But so many people have become Muslim through such-and-such!" we say. As if Allah guiding a person in the worst of circumstances points to the greatness of the circumstance, and not the greatness of Allah. *SubhaanAllah.*

Undoubtedly, Allah choosing to guide a person to Islam through us is one of the greatest honors in this world. However, we should not allow this divine decision to make us fall into self-deception. The truth of Islam is so clear that the signs of its truth are everywhere, even in places of evil and corruption. This is because the entire earth belongs to Allah, and everything and everyone on it points to His Oneness and Glory—even those ignorant enough to think it is *their* glory that points people to Him.

Idols.

In the religion of emotionalism, where hurt feelings equal wrongdoing and emotional desires equal ultimate good, I'm always amazed by whose feelings we ultimately choose to measure wrongdoing, and whose feelings we pretend don't exist.

Naturally, every human has feelings, so a culture of emotionalism is valid only insomuch as we measure right and wrong based on the feelings of everyone equally. However, this isn't what we do.

Instead, we assign ourselves and those *we* care about as the only humans on earth. We then proceed with our self-serving principles of emotionalism to accuse others of wronging us and those we care about.

That it never occurs to us to apply our principles from the opposite vantage point (i.e. in the experience of those we accuse of wrongdoing) suggests that it isn't hurt feelings or emotional desires that we are using to measure right and wrong.

It is ourselves—whom we've effectively placed as a god above everyone else.

~

Every nation has the one idol that they don't want to give up. Ours is human emotions and desires.

And nowhere is this *shirk* more obvious than in our marriages (in how we seek to control our husbands and wives) and in how we view others' sexuality when it violates the Book of Allah.

Every argument we have boils down to how someone *feels* or what they want—except when someone feels genuine *emaan* and wants to obey Allah.

Then and only then do we say feelings and desires should be ignored. Because the religion of emotions and desires dictates that the only unforgivable sin is to put God before anything else.

Fire.

Are you ready for the fire?
I don't mean the fire that burns due to punishment.
I mean the fire that burns due to faith.
That fire—that *fitnah*—that burns through every belief you've claimed, every word you've spoken, and every good deed you *think* you've done.
It is the burning trial our Lord has written for everyone who claims belief on their tongue.
It separates the truthful from the deceivers, the strong from the weak, and the believers from the hypocrites.
Are you ready?
Its blaze reaches us in the privacy of our homes, in the public platforms of our social media, and under the warm limelight of praise and self-satisfaction.
And it burns where we're least aware—and our only armor and fortification are what lies deepest in our hearts.
But do you even know what's there?
You get a glimpse each time you are asked to speak the truth about Allah's religion, yet the answer goes against your deepest desires of life and heart.
And dear soul, what will you say?
The answer can help answer, Are you ready the fire?

> "Do people think that they will be left alone on saying, 'We believe' and that they will not be tested? We did test those before them, and Allah will certainly make known those who are true from those who are liars."
> —Qur'an, *Al-'Ankaboot* (29:2-3)

Nothing quiets conviction like living the very circumstance you thought you knew so much about.

~

Have you ever heard of a more heartbreaking phenomenon than Muslims fighting Islam?

~

It is one thing to acknowledge that all humans, in theory, are subject to error and thus are in need of guidance and direction. But it is another thing entirely to apply that theory to your own reality, then face it head on with humility.

Just as there are non-Muslims who will die having never heard of Islam in a true and correct way, there are Muslims who will die having never heard of Islam in a true and correct way.

And just as there are non-Muslims who know in their heart the truth of Islam but will meet their death rejecting it, there are Muslims who know in their heart the true and correct understanding of Islam but dedicate their lives to rejecting it in favor of their own desires, opinions, and ideas.

Balance.

When faced with spiritual turmoil or confusion, we're often told to "be safe"—to follow the path that protects oneself from misguidance and doubt; and we assume this means following the strictest opinions.
But religious safety isn't what exhausts the soul and confounds the mind. It is what gives the soul peace and the mind clarity— and inspires one to not only follow the guidance of the Qur'an and Sunnah, but to love doing so.

~

Except for the foundational and clear matters in Islam that are not subject to permissible disagreement, there is no "one size fits all" way to practice this faith. So it's wisest to limit your Islamic teachings and "commanding the good and forbidding the evil" to the foundational and clear teachings of Allah and His Messenger (peace be upon him) instead of your personal opinions and convictions and the inflexible views of your preferred group and religious teacher.

Disagreements are not only a part of life, but they are also *necessary* and healthy to optimal spiritual, psychological, and emotional growth. If you seek to eliminate all disagreement from religious contexts, it is not Islam you wish to implement. Rather, it is oppression and religious extremism—no matter how convinced you are that you are right.

So now Muslims are claiming that some people aren't obligated to believe in Allah's Book and Messengers in order to enter Paradise—and that these people can disbelieve in the Qur'an and Prophet Muhammad (peace be upon him) and still be counted as believers in front of Allah. *SubhaanAllah*.

Believing in Allah could *never* be synonymous with disbelief. When the Qur'an mentions those who believe in Allah and the Last Day as having their reward, please know that the key word here is "believe." And all spiritual belief comes with conditions, as both divine texts and common sense make obvious.

Ignorance of certain prophets and revelations—or living in a time before they came—is completely different from knowing of them yet *choosing* to reject them.

Allah says, "And whoever seeks a religion other than Islam, never will it be accepted of him, and in the Hereafter he will be of those who have lost [all spiritual good]" (3:85).

Yes, our faith recognizes that there are people who lived (and continue to live) and never heard of Islam or Prophet Muhammad, peace be upon him. But our Lord making excuses for sincere ignorance is not the same as Him exempting His slaves from the obligation of belief altogether. Such an allowance has never existed since the beginning of time, and it will never exist until the End of Time.

Immodesty.

SubhaanAllah.
Is following the faults of women now the sixth pillar of Islam? No matter how much some Muslims study this beautiful faith, they still come away with this bizarre manmade "principle of *fiqh*": Any action by a woman that even has the *possibility* to involve the eyes or ears of men is by default evil and a sign of corruption and immodesty on her part.
So now we have to read endless posts about the decision of a *hijabi* or *niqaabi* to post a picture, to do an online hijab tutorial, or to even recite Qur'an!
By Allah, I've even seen some women change the required *Salaah* movements to appease the *possible* wicked thoughts of men.
Laa ilaaha illaAllah! What is wrong with us?
Even in the face of apparent wrong, we are taught to make excuses for our brothers and sisters.
Must we be taught the same regarding the apparent *good* of believing women, since we now twist nearly every public deed of theirs to be evil?

~

Men, I have my own soul to fend for, so please leave me alone to do it. Excuse my bluntness, but I couldn't care less about any *fitnah* you face as a result of my speech or actions when I am doing nothing displeasing to Allah.
So here's my advice: Be a man.
Can you do that?
Men lower their gazes and focus on their own souls.
If that's too hard for you, then at least keep quiet about your personal problems. They have nothing to do with me.

If you truly believe polygyny is *haraam* in today's society because it doesn't comprise a "legal marriage" in the West, do you also believe it's *haraam* to enter into monogamy based on a *nikaah* (Islamic marriage) alone?

Keep in mind, by definition, *haraam* means an act that holds the punishment of Hellfire in the Hereafter.

But I've never heard of Allah threatening His servants with torment in the Hereafter for obeying Him, whether through a *nikaah* or anything else. This, irrespective of how disbelievers define marriage—a definition that, by the way, has nothing whatsoever to do with the meaning of *"nikaah"* in Islam.

Nor with criminalizing the use of certain religious *vocabulary* to describe the private decisions of consenting adults.

But I *have* heard of our Lord threatening us—quite severely in fact—should we ever have the audacity to speak a lie about the religion then attribute it to Him.

In fact, it is considered an act of *shirk* to knowingly make the *halaal haraam*, or to knowingly follow a religious leader in this.

Is it not sufficient that Allah has given us all choice in how we live out our private lives? Why must we risk throwing away our very souls—by using religion as a smokescreen to hide our hatred for parts of the very religion we claim?

Showing not even the slightest disturbance in the face of clear wrongdoing is neither humility nor good character. But we've somehow convinced ourselves that emotional impotence equals piety. So a million wrongs can unfold before us, yet we sit idly by saying, "I place my trust in Allah."
If that were really true, then you'd *do* something about the wrong you see.
Tawakkul is not passivity.
It is the courage to speak up when others are silent, the motivation to act while others sit still, and the restless determination to set matters right when things are wrong.

~

Life is a continuous internal struggle for both patience and gratitude. When you have a healthy balance of both, trusting Allah comes quite naturally.

~

Dear every hater, controller, abuser, and envious eye.
You helped create the pain that became my power.
So thank you. I am stronger because of you.
With your love and support, I would never be where I am today. So I'm grateful that you withheld it, and forced upon me *tawakkul* (trust in God) instead.

Tawakkul.

I think our enemies are sent to beautify our hearts, fortify our spirits, and cleanse our souls.

~

Spiritual tranquility is not a passive state of mystic calm. It is a heart at rest after having done all the hard, necessary, grinding work that your Lord requires of believers on earth. Anything else is cowardice and laziness, no matter the "pious" spin you put on your refusal to actively work against the wrongs within you and around you.

Tranquility.

Activism.

Community work begins with the heart.
And I'm not talking about only our own.
Any activism not rooted in calling people to tend to their hearts—by fulfilling their most fundamental purpose on earth: worshiping and obeying God alone—is bound to be rooted in emotionalism more than social justice.
Emotionalism inspires us to follow the faults of others, while social justice inspires us to support the work of others, even if it looks different from our own—because everyone has a role to play, whether a mother in her home, a father feeding his family, a protester in a peaceful march, or a preacher or imam on the pulpit. This is a fundamental principle of any successful community activism.

True activists understand that a community is made up of necessary parts in a complex puzzle, and no piece is devalued, including (and most especially) the parts only God can see. Because to discount the human good you cannot see is to discount the favor of God that you hope to see.

~

Any activism not rooted in calling people to tend to their hearts is bound to be fraught with reckless emotionalism, destructive narcissism, and following the faults of anyone whose life work looks different from yours.

~

If you don't care about the human soul, you don't care about human life. It really is that simple.
So to speak about human rights while trampling upon the human soul—yours or anyone else's—is a violation of the very rights you claim to stand for.

Politics.

What right do you have to harass the people of the cave, when Allah praises them in Qur'an?

On whose authority do you speak ill of those who retreat from corrupt social and political systems and opt not to participate at all—out of fear for their souls? Are you certain that those you call "lazy" or "ignorant" are not written down as beloved to Allah? Were the youth who retreated to the cave lazy and ignorant—or were they wise and faithful?

No, not every wise and faithful servant of Allah who is praised in His Book rushed to the shelter of a cave to worship Him. But the ones we are instructed to read about every Friday did retreat from a corrupt society over which they had no control. So consider carefully the Divine reason for this weekly reading before you harass those who only wish to worship their Lord in peace.

~

If your political view—which allows you to openly support those who oppose your religion—has resulted in you cutting off relationships with those who believe in your religion, then know you are no longer involved in politics. You are involved in sin and wrongdoing.

History.

"We're nothing like them!" we say when we speak of the Prophet, *sallallaahu'alayhi wa sallam*, his Companions, and other righteous believers praised in Qur'an and hadith.

But why are we so eager to separate ourselves from them, when Allah Himself points to them as our example?

And when Allah commands us in every obligatory *Salaah* to pray to be on the Straight Path that they adhered to in their lives?

What then do you think is the purpose of their example, and of this prayer?

Do we really imagine that our brothers and sisters who preceded us couldn't possibly relate to the challenges we face today? Do we really imagine that we can find absolutely nothing in their lives to help us understand our own?

Yet we, like they did before us, face the believers' timeless struggle of holding on to the truth while nearly everything around us—from our *nafs* to the oppressive society in which we live—seeks to pull us away from Allah's Straight Path.

Or do we rush to separate ourselves from their faithful existence because, deep down, we know our dilemmas are no different? Yet the claim of separation allows us to ignore (or deny) our religious obligations, claiming we live in "modern times"? When in fact, *every* era of people lived in modern times, as there is no other possibility for those who are alive during a period in time.

I wonder then what we think we are supposed to learn—other than history—from reading about the youth of the cave, about the plight of those persecuted by Pharaoh, about the *hijrah* from Makkah to Abyssinia and then Madinah? And about every generation calling its people to Allah. What do you think, dear soul?

Are these merely "tales of the ancients"?

Or is possible that, within these stories, there are solutions that our Lord wants us to implement today?

Know the difference between those dedicated to protecting the Muslim image, and those dedicated to protecting the Muslims. They are not the same.

~

Those dedicated to protecting the Muslim image will allow (and even sometimes support) harm to come to Muslims, so long as their coveted image is protected. Those dedicated to protecting the Muslims focus only on the image Allah has of them.

Image.

Adab.

Justice before *adab*.
Yes, we hear "*adab* before knowledge," but when someone has been terribly wronged and they speak up about it, justice comes before good manners and etiquette. They have every right to be outraged, and we have no right to police their words, so long as they're not harming anyone.
It is ridiculous to speak about *adab* after a child has been viciously abused, a woman has been sexually assaulted or raped, or a man's life is in ruins after being falsely accused. Is their tone of speech and word choice really more important than their right to justice?

I find it very interesting that the demand for *adab* often comes from the same camp as the injustice itself. This is true for social-political crimes, and it is true for religious ones. How often are we required to sit in utter "respectful" silence and listen to religious leaders speak lies about our religion, sometimes going as far as to condemn us to Hellfire or to declare that our personal *halaal* choices are *haraam*, often breaking up families as a result?

So no, I will not sit idly in "respectful silence" exercising this narrow definition of *adab*—which really just means giving oppressors free rein to ruin our lives without as much as a word being spoken against them.

Righteous Lies.

The worst opinion is the one in which you lie to yourself and others, and then attribute it to God.
If you're too lazy to pray, be honest with yourself, instead of saying prayer doesn't make someone Muslim. It does.
Prophet Muhammad, peace be upon him, taught that *Salaah* is the dividing line between faith and disbelief.
If you're too weak to wear hijab, be honest about your struggles—we're all human after all—but don't say hijab isn't important in Islam. Our Lord doesn't speak trivialities.
If He spoke about it, it's important.
If you don't want your husband or wife to divorce you, then be honest about your deepest desires and vulnerabilities—we all have them—but don't slander your husband or wife, saying they are bad Muslims to even want this.
If you are too spiritually weak or ignorant to understand the wisdom of polygyny for all times—we all have much to learn about our faith—then pray that Allah increases you in knowledge and understanding.
But don't say polygyny is *haraam* in today's society.
Obeying Allah through marriage is never forbidden, no matter what society you live in.
But lying on Allah is *always* forbidden, no matter your motivation or excuse.
Allah says, **"Woe to those who write the Book with their own hands and then say, 'This is from Allah!'"** (2:79).
Be careful.
Allah has already spoken about prayer, hijab, and marriage.
Limit your "opinion" to His revelation.
Or await facing Him alone on the Day of Judgment,
when you'll be asked to explain why you felt you knew better than He.

Qualifications.

"He's not a scholar anyway!" we often say to dismiss someone's Islamic perspective.
But here's my question: Does it even matter?
Our priority should be gaining the tools to distinguish truth from falsehood—for the sake of our souls—not obsessing over someone's Islamic "qualifications." It's counterintuitive to debate who is or who isn't a scholar when it's our *lack of knowledge* that makes us need a scholar in the first place. Exactly what knowledge are we using to draw a conclusion? And since scholars themselves are debating this question, the answer becomes a rather obviously moot point.

Here's the bottom line: If religious truth comes from the mouth of a layperson, are we allowed to dismiss it? And if religious falsehood comes from the mouth of a scholar, are we obligated to follow it?

Allah placed us on this earth to worship and obey Him, period. And He didn't make this obligation hidden in rocket science or brainteasers. So as long as your heart is sincere and you consistently turn to Him for guidance, He makes the truth clear so that you follow it, and He makes falsehood clear so that you avoid it. This is the case whether you're a layperson or scholar. And no, no guarantee of guidance or misguidance exists for either.
Thus, whether or not so-and-so qualifies to be called a "scholar" really shouldn't be our concern. But whether or not *we* are qualified to enter Paradise, this should be.

"But we need scholars to help us!" you say. And I agree. On this, I share this lesson from our pious predecessors: Take your knowledge from those who have passed away [i.e. the Prophet (peace be upon him) and his Companions], for their knowledge and righteousness are well known. As for the men and women amongst you today, you do not know their affair in front of Allah, and you do not know in what spiritual state they will die. So take from them only what you recognize [as truth], and leave what you cannot verify [as truth].

And Allah is All-Forgiving, Most Merciful to His slaves.

Bliss.

Ignorance is perhaps bliss—but only for those afflicted with ignorance. It is the informed who suffer from the "bliss" of others.

~

"Just be yourself!" is the advice given to everyone, except those who see the "self" in full submission to God.

Our Focus.

"Ask them how much Qur'an they've memorized!"
I think it's time we stop using the perceived faults of others to justify our points of view on controversial issues.
If we believe that music is generally forbidden or allowed, or that the face veil is obligatory or optional, it should be because we genuinely believe this view is most strongly supported by divine evidence—not because we're able to enumerate the faults of those with a different point of view.

Personally, I've been blessed to study Qur'an from some of the most knowledgeable teachers, and there is not a single controversial point of view that they all shared.
Yes, I've had Qur'an teachers who listened to music and those who didn't, those who favored covering the face and those who wore a simple hijab and colorful clothes.
But the one trait they all shared, without exception, was their general humility in speaking about Allah—and about their brothers and sisters in Islam.

This experience taught me that the true sign of Qur'an entering our hearts is in how it corrects our speech and behavior, and how it increases our love and compassion for fellow believers, despite their faults and varying points of view.

And one of the most glaring signs of a sick heart in need of Qur'an is that we actually imagine that our ability to count the faults of others somehow proves we're on the right path. Yet all this proves is that we've tragically missed the most basic message of Qur'an itself: humbly turning to Allah for guidance and forgiveness—and focusing on our own souls.

Ihsaan.

From the Journal of Umm Zakiyyah

Jihaad al-nafs.

Islam is submission, yes.
But it is more than that.
It is a relentless fight till death—against oneself—to save one's soul.

~

You can beat them—and join them—by making your fight the one within yourself.

~

It is not that I do not love anything of this world.
It's just that nothing of this world loves me.
So why give my heart to one who'll ultimately cast me aside?

We, this modern generation, are a people who love injustice so long as we are the ones inflicting it. Our cries against wrongdoing are loud and clear when it is our lives touched by harm. But when we see some worldly benefit for ourselves, we rush to inflict harm on others then declare that it is our right. So amongst us are those who stand up to fight racism then declare their own people are superior in the eyes of God.
And amongst us are men who speak openly about their rights in the home then prevent their wives from having even minds of their own.
And amongst us are women who speak openly about their rights in marriage, yet keep their children from their own fathers in the case of divorce.
And amongst us are those who fight for the right of everyone to marry whom they chose, then verbally abuse virgin women who prefer older men, or any man or woman who chooses polygyny.
And amongst us are parents who speak endlessly about their God-given rights to obedience and respect, yet they make their children's lives hell if they so much as hold an Islamic view or personal opinion that differs from them.
And the list goes on and on.
And then we sit and genuinely wonder why corruption and injustice are widespread in the world, while we need only to look honestly at how we behave in our homes and with our tongues and social media accounts—when encountering something *we* dislike.
The true measure of fighting injustice is not when you are suffering harm and you speak up against it, but when you are gaining worldly benefit when someone else is suffering harm, yet you sacrifice your own personal opinions, desires, and worldly comforts in the pursuit of what is right before God.

Dhulm.

Choose your advisors carefully, especially when it comes to important decisions like marriage.

In general there are two categories of people who offer advice on marriage: those who trust Allah, and those who trust themselves.

Advisors who trust Allah will *always* encourage you to consult your Lord before making any decision, and they will openly acknowledge that only you, with the help of Allah, can ultimately determine what is best for you. Yes, they will also let you know the pros and cons of certain life choices so that you can, *bi'idhnillaah*, make an informed, wise decision that is best for your life and soul. But they will *never* seek to define marital happiness for you.

Those who trust themselves will list for you a million don'ts, many of which fall in the category of what is permissible and beloved to Allah. And their advice is almost always rooted in their own insecurities. They will tell you not to marry into a certain race, color or income bracket, and they'll have a million opinions against "settling" for someone who's divorced, in polygyny, has children—and the list goes on and on.

Because their insecurities go on and on.

Yes, we all have insecurities.

But unless you're seeking to have someone else's added your own, then choose the advisor who trusts Allah.

It will encourage you to do the same.

~

If you—whether layperson or scholar—interpret nearly every verse of admonition or warning in the Qur'an as addressing someone else, then know you are interpreting it incorrectly, and perhaps dangerously.

First and foremost, the Book of Allah is a direct message from your Lord to you specifically, for the sake of saving *your own* soul. Yes, it also includes instructions to remind and warn others—but only after you've made a lifelong commitment of focusing on His Words as a means to check yourself.

All this obsessing about the need to praise certain people is exhausting.
I feel much more peaceful and inspired when I focus on my ever-present need to praise Allah.

~

Students of misguidance are taught to not question human beings. Students of spiritual truth are taught to not question Allah.

Al-Hamd.

'Ulamaa.

Religious knowledge is rooted more in the heart than in the mind. As such, when Allah speaks about the *'ulamaa*, people of knowledge, He speaks about their fear of Him, not their accolades and certificates from books, classes, and teachers. Allah says, "It is only those who fear Allah, amongst His slaves, who are *'ulamaa*" (*Al-Faatir*, 35:28).
Thus, our classes and teachers—and accolades and certifications—benefit us only insomuch as our hearts benefit us.

Reflect, O child of Adam, reflect!
Then repent and self-correct.

If the child of Adam knew his account of every wrong he's done to himself and others, he wouldn't be so quick to become angry at others' wrongs toward him. Instead, he'd rush to forgive them in hopes that Allah would forgive him.

~

So many of us feel that we've finally found that one sheikh or group that will protect us from misguidance. Yet ironically, the main reason we feel secure is that most of our time is spent focusing on the wrongs of *other* groups, thus making us blind to the potential wrongs of our own.

~

Today I focus on neither blame nor forgiveness regarding those who have hurt me.
I focus on only healing.
And I leave it to God to take account of their deeds.

Al-Hisaab.

Al-Lisaan.

Mind your business.
These three words can be life savers, and soul savers too.

~

The tongue, O Allah, the tongue!
Protect me from it, even as it moves in broken rhythm with my own troubled heart.

~

"Travel and tell no one. Live a true love story and tell no one. Live happily and tell no one. People ruin beautiful things."
—**Khalil Gibran**

This, my friends, is why I'm silent on so much of my life. People think that once your story is put to words or paper, they can give it a rating, as if experience begs for input or approval—or lack thereof.
So live quietly in gratefulness.
The tongue of the human is a weapon, and it can slice through even the most intangible of good.

~

A tongue that moves in exposing the faults of people is a tongue supplicating to Allah to expose his own—and a tongue that moves in covering the faults of people is a tongue supplicating to Allah to cover his own.

Here's the bottom line, there are just some things you'd *never* do to or say about someone you genuinely love and care about, especially publicly and online—and then go on to mention them *by name*—especially when your outrage is concerning a situation that has a much less incriminating explanation than what you're portraying.
This isn't warning about evil.
This is spreading evil.

By Allah! I don't know what mental or spiritual place a Muslim must be in to rush to disobey Allah and His Messenger, *sallallaahu'alayhi wa sallam*, by having no mercy on their fellow believers when they see something they disagree with.

O Allah, return us to your Religion! O Allah, return us to your Religion! And O Allah, put love and mercy in our hearts for each other, and guard our tongues from uttering anything that displeases You! And O Allah, forgive our sins and protect our hearts from arrogance, our tongues from lying, and our faith and actions from misguidance!

We want the one correcting us to have compassion and wisdom and to understand that no one is perfect. Yet our frustration with them proves we do not understand this point ourselves. For if we did, we'd apply this principle to them, just as we demand that they apply it to us—and we'd show compassion and understanding when we see their faults as they encourage us toward good.
Like us, they are not perfect.
They are merely a mirror of ourselves.

~

I too believe in discussing what is happening in the world. I just view "giving glad tidings to the believers" to be more emphasized in our faith and more urgent in our times.

~

I wonder why our hearts feel more strongly the obligation to say when our Muslim brothers and sisters are wrong than the obligation to protect their honor and reputation, whether they're right or wrong.

Hikmah.

When I see a person praying, I see a person praying, and I want to encourage that, no matter what sins they are obviously struggling with.

We all have sins, and it breaks my heart that we have Muslims making so many of us feel like we should abandon prayer "out of respect for Allah" if we find ourselves in an un-ideal location or sinful situation when the prayer time arrives.

This is a perspective I've never read or heard in the Qur'an, Sunnah, or the life of the Companions. To me, it sounds like the whispering of Shaytaan.

Personally, I cannot fathom how anyone who believes in Allah and the Last Day can be disturbed by the sight of a believer bowing to his Lord in prayer, no matter the location.

Yes, I hate to see them in a sinful situation, but I *love* to see them praying despite that.

May Allah have mercy on them and forgive them, as at least they know Whom to turn to for help.

— in response to comments on my blog "He Prayed in a Club!"

Are you minding your business or someone else's?
While it might be your business to remind others about Allah, it's not your business to define what that relationship will look like for them.
So if you're "correcting" people on matters that are subject to permissible disagreement, chances are, you're minding someone else's business instead of your own.

~

You are not me, and I am not you. We are not cookie cutters of each other, so let's remember that when telling others what they should and should not do, especially regarding matters subject to permissible disagreement.
I find it quite telling and profound that the foundational, clear, and undisputed matters in our faith are very few in comparison to the ever-growing list of issues subject to scholarly disagreement, personal circumstance, and individual choice. It tells me that my Lord is *Al-'Aleem, Al-Hakeem*—All-Knowing, All-Wise—in giving us a religion that can be applied to every circumstance, every people, every culture, and every generation till the end of time.

But as has been the case of both social and political tyrants in history, there are always people who believe they know better than God. These people believe the All-Powerful, All-Aware needs our help more than we need His, so they use the faculties that God has given them to inform Him and His servants about issues that He apparently overlooked. For these people, the concept of permissible disagreement does not exist—and often the concept of impermissible disagreement also does not exist. For them, their mind processes only one inflexible perspective on every religious issue: "mine."

Ikhlaas.

The greatest act of selflessness is to put your soul before anything else—including, and most especially, yourself.

~

Everyone who openly disagrees with you is not a "hater," and everyone who openly agrees with you is not a friend. Some disagreement is rooted in love, and some agreement merely masks animosity rusting in the heart. The former reflects the heart of a believer, the latter the heart of a hypocrite.

May Allah purify our hearts and write us down amongst the sincere.

~

If you want to know life's ultimate joy, then find contentment in that which is between only you and your Lord.

O Allah! How does anyone survive in this world without consulting You before making a decision?

~

You can't be everything to everybody.
You can't even be everything to yourself.
So delegate.
You can't do this alone.
Give your problems to Allah.

Istikhaarah.

Da'wah, whether to those unfamiliar with spiritual truth or to Muslims who prefer this world over the Hereafter, is a delicate balance between sincere, consistent inviting, and prioritizing your own soul and well-being over anyone else's. The fact of the matter is, for the vast majority of humans on earth, all of the good, happiness, and success they strive for will end in the grave—even as they know full well the reality of returning to their Creator. And no matter how much you love and care for them, there's nothing you can do or say to make them want the good. For this world is too endearing to them, and they refuse to let it go, even as their most coveted convictions and desires will expire with them.
So yes, invite them to care for their souls, but focus on saving your own. They made their choice, and you made yours. So dedicate your life to attaining ultimate spiritual good, because stressing over others could lead you to sacrifice even that.

~

It is indeed an amazing phenomenon, the disbelieving soul.
It throws itself away and hungrily accepts nothing in return,
Except a bed of dirt
And a torment that never ends.

~

The greatest gift you can give humanity is the truth.

Remaining grateful doesn't necessarily mean always being positive, and being positive doesn't necessarily mean always feeling happy. Gratefulness is more a way of life rooted in faith in God than it is the experience of never feeling distressed about life's severe trials or negative circumstances.
Yes, gratefulness requires a level of underlying positivity, but it doesn't require complete positivity. While negativity should never be allowed to define us, feeling moments of negativity is natural and unavoidable. This doesn't make you ungrateful. It makes you human.
And one of the surest ways to destroy both gratefulness and happiness is to deny your right to being human.

~

In my life, I'm finding that it is gratefulness—in its truest form—that is most difficult to sustain.

~

The greatest agonies of life are felt when the eyes and heart long for what is not their own. Then they lament the loss of what never belonged to them in the first place.

Gratefulness, sincerity, and humility.
These are the three most difficult traits to achieve,
and subsequently hold on to in life.

~

Dear soul full of hope and fear,
you are already victorious.
You need only to be patient until you see the fruits of your
good end.

Shahaadah.

What is it that you want from life?

This is a question we all must ask ourselves if we want to benefit from our time on earth.

But too few of us have the only answer that makes sense: fulfilling our purpose of creation by believing in God and submitting to Him.

For many, the answer will be merely grasping some worldly happiness that they'll be compelled to let go of once they are lowered beneath the ground.

But for most people, I don't think they really know.

They're too busy living life—and don't realize that, even if you've never asked yourself this question, everything you do is a testimony to your answer.

Whatever corruption is in your soul is your own doing.
No amount of aggression, abuse or wrongdoing grants
anyone access to your soul. So if something is wrong there,
it is because of your own sicknesses and sins,
not anyone else's.

~

Satan cannot reach us unless there's an opening.
So when we face our human weaknesses and sins, let's not
dismiss them by saying, "That's *Shaytaan*"—but instead focus
on finding the opening in ourselves and lives that allowed
him in.

Tazkiyah.

Missed prayers are missed opportunities.
And no, I don't mean only for your soul in the Hereafter.
I mean also for your life in this world.
Prayer clears the sight, mind, and heart such that you can see, perceive, and understand worldly blessings when they come to you. Abandoning prayer is abandoning reason and common sense. It blocks your sight, mind, and heart from even recognizing what is happening right in front of you, good or bad.
So yes, missed prayers are missed opportunities.
What a tragedy life is for those who will taste neither the sweetness of this world nor the sweetness of the Hereafter. They live a miserable, discontented life devoid of blessings, then they die and live a miserable, agonizing existence for all eternity.
And to think, it all could have been avoided had they taken the opportunity for blessings when they were called to Islam and prayer.
But they refused.
What a tragic missed opportunity indeed.

Dear soul, know this, and know it well. You are never safe.
It doesn't matter what group you've attached to, what
spiritual teacher praises you, or what praiseworthy label
you've put on yourself. You have no guarantee of
protection from misguidance or even disbelief.
In fact, we are most susceptible to these spiritual tragedies
when we think we are safe from them.
Remember, it was arrogance and self-satisfaction that
destroyed Iblis, not attaching himself to the wrong group,
teacher, or label.
But no one and nothing—and I mean absolutely no one and
nothing—can do your soul-work on your behalf.
Have faith, yes, but do not become comfortable.
Until your soul is seized and you have received the glad
tidings that your Lord is pleased with you,
you are *never* safe.

~

There is nothing in this world for me, except the
opportunity to leave it in peace—and find that my Lord is
pleased with me.

Al-Khaashi'oon

"And seek help in patience and *As-Salaah* (the prayer), and truly it is extremely heavy and hard except for *Al-Khaashi'oon* (the humbly submissive)."
—Qur'an (*Al-Baqarah*, 2:45)

~

"The Religion is easy. So whoever overburdens himself in his religion will not be able to continue in that way. So you should not go to extremes, rather strive to be near perfection. Receive good tidings that you will be rewarded, and gain strength by offering the prayers in the mornings, afternoons, and during the last hours of the nights."
—Prophet Muhammad, peace be upon him (Bukhari)

~

O Allah! Write us down amongst the Khaashi'oon, and make our comfort and joy the Salaah! And purify our hearts, forgive our sins, and cover our faults! And help us do the deeds that are pleasing to You until we meet You!

Also By Umm Zakiyyah

Pain. From the Journal of Umm Zakiyyah
Broken yet Faithful. From the Journal of Umm Zakiyyah
Let's Talk About Sex and Muslim Love
UZ Short Story Collection
The Test Paper (children's book)
If I Should Speak
A Voice
Footsteps
Realities of Submission
Hearts We Lost
The Friendship Promise
Muslim Girl
His Other Wife

Order information available at ummzakiyyah.com/store

Glossary of Arabic Terms.

adab: good manners and etiquette
Ahlul-Qiblah: the people who face Makkah in prayer
Al-Haadiy: The Guide (Name of Allah)
al-hamd: the praise
al-hisaab: the reckoning or being called to account
al-khaashi'oon: those who are humbly submissive
al-lisaan: the tongue
Al-Wadood: The Loving One (Name of Allah)
Al-Wahhaab: The Bestower of Good (Name of Allah)
'aql: human intelligence or common sense
Ar-Rahmaan: The Merciful, Most Gracious (Name of Allah)
Ar-Razzaaq: The Provider (Name of Allah)
ayaat: parts of Qur'an or signs of Allah (God)
bi'idhnillaah: with the help of Allah
da'wah: inviting others to Islam or teaching about Islam
dhikr: remembrance of Allah
dhulm: wrongdoing or oppression
du'aa: prayerful supplication
emaan: faith or spiritual belief
fiqh: scholarly interpretation of Islamic jurisprudence
fitnah: severe trial or temptation
furqaan: criterion of judgment distinguishing right from wrong
halaal: permissible
hasad: harmful jealousy or envy
haraam: forbidden
hijabi: a woman who reveals only her face and hands
hijrah: migration
hikmah: wisdom
husnul-dhann: the best assumption or benefit of the doubt
ihsaan: the highest excellence in worshipping Allah
ijmaa': religious issue involving no historic disagreement
ikhlaas: sincerity or seeking Allah's pleasure alone
ikhtilaaf: disagreement or difference of opinion
Istikhaarah: formal prayer for making a decision
Jannah: Paradise
jihaad al-nafs: internal battle of the self against the self
khushoo': sincere and humble concentration and reflection
kibr: pride or arrogance
Laa ilaaha illaAllah: Nothing has the right to be worshipped except God alone
libaas: garment or clothing (used in reference to a spouse)
madh-hab: school of thought
nafs: the self
naseehah: advice given with sincerity and hope for good
nikaah: Islamic marriage
niqaabi: a woman who wears a face veil
Qiyaam al-Layl: the voluntary night prayer
rahmah: mercy
Sahaabah: Companions of Prophet Muhammad, peace be upon him
Salaah (or As-Salaah): formal prayer
salaf: first three generations of Muslims
sallallaahu'laayhi wa sallam: peace and blessings upon him
shahaadah: formal testimony of truth and Oneness of God
Shaytaan: Satan

shirk: assigning divine attributes to creation or creation's attributes to God
shukr: gratefulness or thankfulness
Siraatul-Mustaqeem: The Straight Path (of spiritual truth)
SubhaanAllah: glorification of Allah
Tahajjud: the voluntary night prayer
tawakkul: sincere trust in or reliance on Allah alone
tawfeeq: enduring firmness upon spiritual truth
tazkiyah: spiritual purification
'ulamaa: scholars or people of knowledge

About the Author

Daughter of American converts to Islam, Umm Zakiyyah (also known by her birth name Ruby Moore), writes about the interfaith struggles of Muslims and Christians, and the intercultural, spiritual, and moral struggles of Muslims in America. Her work has earned praise from writers, professors, and filmmakers and has been translated into multiple languages.

To find out more about the author, visit ummzakiyyah.com or uzauthor.com, subscribe to her YouTube channel: uzreflections, follow her on Twitter and Instagram: uzauthor, or join her Facebook page at facebook.com/ummzakiyyahpage.

www.ingramcontent.com/pod-product-compliance
Lightning Source LLC
Chambersburg PA
CBHW051345040426
42453CB00007B/411